Of Markets and Men

Reshaping finance for a new season

James Featherby

First published in 2012

Published by the Centre for Tomorrow's Company with The Institute of Chartered Accountants in England and Wales and the London Institute for Contemporary Christianity

Centre for Tomorrow's Company
Registered office: Samuel House
6 St Alban's Street, London SW1Y 4SQ
Charity registration number 1055908

ISBN: 978-0-9572949-1-2

FSC
www.fsc.org

RECYCLED

Paper made from
recycled material

FSC® C022913

The paper used in this publication:

– Contains material sources from responsibly
  managed and sustainable commercial
  forests, certified in accordance with the
  FSC (Forest Stewardship Council);

– Is made using 100% recycled post-consumer
  content, reducing the impact of landfill and
  energy consumption.

Designed and produced by studio401

Dedicated to

Joseph Featherby
1930-2010

A relationship banker, inter-generational thinker and committed gardener

Acknowledgements

Nothing is achieved without the contribution of others. I would like to thank the Tomorrow's Company team, including Tony Manwaring, who has done so much to help bring this book to fruition, Pat Cleverly and Anahide Pilibossian, as well as Richard Spencer at ICAEW and Mark Greene at LICC and their teams, for their commitment to this publication; Slaughter and May, and its partners and clients, for all that they taught me; and the many others who have stirred my thinking through the example of their lives, the insights they have shared with me or the books they have written. I would also like to thank my friends, at home and in the City, who have so graciously supported me for so many years in what, for some, has seemed such a foreign working environment. In this regard, my particular thanks go to Rachel Blanshard, Laurence Singlehurst and Trevor Withers. Most of all, however, my thanks go to my wife Charlotte and our five children John, Thomas, Amy, Joshua, and Rose for putting up with the difficulties, providing great wisdom and sharing the fun.

Contents

Preface

"Ideas have legs" – one of James' favourite phrases. This book is a testament to the belief in the power of ideas to create a more constructive, just and humane world. To question basic assumptions, to shed new light, to question the foundations of our thinking, and in so doing to help us re-think how we might better achieve our purpose, rooted in clear values and strong ethical foundations.

This book is also deeply personal to James – it is in a very real sense a 'love letter to the City' from someone who has enjoyed a successful career working in the City at one of its most prestigious law firms, and who, as a leading corporate lawyer, has got to know the City and all of its workings from the 'inside out'. James challenges the City to play its fullest possible role as part of the nation, a City we can all be proud of, truly productive, contributing to the common good at the same time as it delivers private benefit.

James ends using the powerful analogy of building a cathedral – a labour of love, spanning generations, building something of enduring value, that changes not just the landscape we see but also the landscape of our mind. Durham Cathedral makes this tangible and real. It is a manifestation of the enormous power of ideas to reshape our reality. Imagine standing in Durham in 1098, witness to the building of a new cathedral. If you had visited other cathedrals of the age you would have expected to see one much like others across the land: Romanesque, heavy, semi-circular, made of huge lumps of stone, and as a result constrained in their height and access to light.

The master masons though had other ideas. They came up with a whole new way of building arches with the result that the cathedral they built could reach new heights – and as each level soared, the spires of Durham Cathedral quite literally touched the heavens. Stone arches seem like a given, immutable, solid, unyielding. But they are not: they are a product of our imagination. In this case, ribbed vaulting, with four crossed ribs that meet together at the centre, where they meet the keystone. New possibilities sprang forth: the vaults could now come to a point, arches became narrower and taller. What was once set in stone took on a whole new meaning. Cathedrals were reshaped and redefined.

When we think about finance, business and society – and the relationship between them – we have come to assume that all of this is indeed set in stone. And perhaps it is; that is, until we find a new keystone.

For that is what James Featherby has given us: a new keystone.

And that is why we are all so proud to be publishing this book: the Institute of Chartered Accountants in England and Wales, the London Institute for Contemporary Christianity and Tomorrow's Company. We each represent different facets of what makes James tick and together, we hope, provide both platform and springboard to do justice to the quality of the ideas he sets out in this book *Of Markets and Men*.

The importance of this keystone lies in both the quality of James' ideas but also in their expression. James builds on his earlier and hugely well received *The White Swan Formula*, written in the wake of the financial crisis, a powerful statement of the importance of a renewal of values as a necessary precondition of the renewal of the City. James I know has been pleasantly surprised by the pace of change, of developments such as the Lord Mayor's Initiative on Restoring Trust in the City; the establishment of the Chartered Banker Professional Standards Board; and of contributions such as Gervais Williams' *Slow Finance*. He shouldn't be, given the powerful contribution he himself has made, alongside many others. But we would agree with James that there is still much to be done.

James won't I hope mind me saying that his response is both analytical and profoundly human. He was I know deeply moved by the crisis not only of confidence but also of self-worth experienced by many in the City as a result of the banking crisis. This was often at great personal, albeit hidden, cost and it cast a powerful shadow over many families. A crisis which now demands clarity of thinking, goodness of heart, and the courage to put forward new ideas and stimulate and reinforce new thinking and conversations if we are now to protect the next generation from the follies of our mistakes.

These qualities shine through from the words on the page. James writes beautifully and economically, at times poetically. In so doing he challenges in practical ways the increasingly individualistic, reductionist, utilitarian, controlling and pragmatic nature of Western thought. It has been a rare but deep honour to witness and at times hopefully support James as he has explored the ideas which have now taken shape in this important book, as he left his former career, exploring with great humility and care his own mandate to develop and share his ideas until, with increasing clarity, the pieces fell into place, the book written.

James puts forward four big ideas: a public purpose for large companies; reducing the burden of debt throughout the economy; challenging financial speculation for its own sake; promoting productive investment for social and environmental as well as financial benefit. In each case he puts forward specific proposals – ideas with legs – that invite deeper consideration, shaping the vaulted arches that might both inspire and bear the weight of mapping a future for business and finance which is, as James says, more relational, holistic, neighbourly, purposeful, adventurous, humble and principled.

To describe this as a new cathedral though is to invite hubris. For as the title of this publication reminds us, in the words of the great Robert Burns, *"The best laid schemes o' Mice an' Men/Go oft awry"*. As James would be the first to say, cathedrals that last require enormous collective effort, over generations. But they need keystones, a role this book is destined to play.

Tony Manwaring
Chief Executive
Tomorrow's Company

July 2012

Foreword

"Capitalism is the worst system, except for all those others…" When Churchill said this he was talking about 'democracy', but we could substitute 'capitalism'.

As citizens we could all just accept that booms and busts in economies and asset markets are part of the capitalist system and a reflection of our 'animal spirits', as John Maynard Keynes put it. Or, hopefully as 'thinking' human beings, we could have the confidence and desire to determine together whether we can make progress in the widest sense. As James so elegantly and provocatively points out in this book, many people have a wide and deep-seated sense of unease relating not only to the credit crunch that we are still 'dealing' with, but perhaps also to broader questions as to the nature of finance and how it relates to our society and the economy more generally.

Each of James' four 'bold steps' would merit a volume in their own right, and no doubt they will do over time. James asks profound questions and suggests some solutions relating to four key areas: first, on the tricky area of the inter-relationship between multinationals and their civic responsibilities; secondly, on the issue of high debt levels across the major areas of the economy; thirdly, some thoughts on financial activity and long-term investing behaviour; and, finally, the challenge of enhancing the link between individual savers, their asset managers and their underlying investments.

Thus, we face a choice. We can 'muddle' through. On the face of it this may appear to be easier than asking ourselves difficult questions – and where solutions may not be easy – preferring to hand over a flawed system to our children and grandchildren. Or, as James suggests, we could respond to the present challenge and try to create significant improvements within the system to the material and spiritual benefit of current and future participants.

As Oscar Wilde said, a cynic is *"someone who knows the price of everything and the value of nothing"*. Let us ensure that finance recovers its sense of values for the benefit of us all.

Edward Bonham Carter
Group Chief Executive
Jupiter Fund Management plc

July 2012

Introduction

It seems strange to me to be writing something that calls for a radical reshaping of the business and financial landscape. I have worked in the City for over 30 years, and I have always believed that business and finance have much to contribute towards building a better world. For most of my career I have, therefore, found myself in conversations with friends defending the City against those who have seen it as the root of all evil. I continue to believe that business and finance have much to contribute. But over the last few decades deep problems have been revealed.

In the 1980s we saw the beginnings of a new form of aggressive capitalism with the arrival of US investment banks and the blurring of the distinction between serving the interests of clients' capital and serving the interests of one's own capital. In the 1990s we saw the build-up to the dotcom bubble and the growth of an investment product sales culture that turned *caveat emptor* (buyer beware) into a licence to make money not only from the foolish but also from those who trusted in the good name of long established institutions. In the 2000s we saw a credit boom develop that injected debt and speculative trading into all of our investment arrangements. And, throughout this period, mega-businesses became ever more powerful on the back of easy credit, a technological revolution and widespread deregulation (including a conspicuous and on-going failure of competition law policy).

Others have been uncomfortable, if not downright critical, of Anglo Saxon capitalism for some time. My own unease has been slower to develop. I remain committed to an enterprise economy. I continue to believe in the power of business to release creativity, create prosperity and support democracy. But it does seem that a finance industry that once served the real economy has inverted that relationship. And that a number of businesses that once served customers have become something of a law unto themselves, impoverishing our social and natural capital in their relentless search for ever increasing growth, even though they may continue to provide us with goods and services that we at least think we need.

Many are calling for a rediscovery of the fact that moral principles, linked to a clear sense of public duty, is the friend not the enemy of business in the long-term. Without morality there is no trust, and without trust there is no business. There is also a causal link between trust and the longer time frames that many now seek for investment perspectives. It is easy to short change clients and customers in the short-term, but more difficult in the long-term. Long-term thinking is not only beneficial for investment, it is vital if one is seeking to build trust.

It is hard, however, to follow positive values when the cards are stacked so heavily against you. I have, therefore, concluded that in some areas radical action is now needed in the shape of regulatory and structural reform; reform that is, I suspect, materially beyond that currently being considered by the Kay Review of UK Equity Markets and Long-term Decision Making.[1]

---

[1] Commissioned by the Secretary of State for Business in June 2011 and due to report finally in the summer of 2012.

Even the reforms I am suggesting, however, would be an insufficient response on their own. The financial crisis is at its core primarily a problem of the human heart, not a technical difficulty. We need a new way of thinking, both collectively and individually. That cannot be achieved through regulation.

I hope what follows sparks your imagination. Often our difficulty is that we believe that things cannot be different. Of course they can be, and the UK excels at creativity. We must imagine a new way of being and of doing, a new kind of future. A desired destination can give us a renewed sense of hope, a clear sense of direction and a store of energy to help us persevere. We may never arrive, at least not this side of heaven, but life is mostly about the journey not the destination.

The market is a useful tool for aggregating and resolving the preferences of many. But it remains only an approximation. The market is like the British justice system. It needs constant attention. It does a job that most of the time is good enough, if not better. But it is never perfect. It makes mistakes, and even when the verdict is right the consequences of the judgement can never entirely satisfy the parties. It delivers justice of a sort, but not perfect justice.

The market is the same. It delivers fairness of a sort, and it helps each of us to trade our surplus time and produce in return for other items that we would prefer. But it always remains subject to the moral requirements of care for the other party to the exchange, care for society, and care for the environment. Markets need to be regulated to remind us of the requirements of justice and the benefits of cooperation, and to provide others with an element of protection against our harmful actions, whether intended or not. At times the rules of the market need to be reset to deliver a better approximation of fairness and care and to address market failures and inefficiencies. Now would be a good time to reset both our rules and our values.

"Creativity is the power to reject the past, to change the status quo, and to seek new potential. Simply put, aside from using one's imagination – and perhaps more importantly – creativity is the power to act. Only through our actions can expectations for change become reality, and only then can our purported creativity build a new foundation, and only then is it possible to draw out human civilization."

Ai Weiwei's Blog
Writings, Interviews, and Digital Rants, 2006-2009

1. Pruning the vine

Rising inequality, unsustainable consumption, unmanageable debt, record employee stress levels, stubbornly high unemployment, environmental degradation, natural resource exhaustion, struggling communities, weakened democracies, ineffective international regulation, impoverished nations, huge trade imbalances. The list could go on.

> "But, Mousie, thou art not alone,
> In proving foresight may be vain:
> The best laid schemes o' Mice an' Men
> Go oft awry,
> And leave us nought but grief an' pain,
> For promised joy."[2]

Capitalism has not fully delivered on all that it promised, and yet an economy based on honest endeavour remains the only way to make economic progress.

It is clear that no one has all the answers. All that any of us can do is tend as best we can the patch of earth that lies before us. So my ambition here is neither to solve all of the world's economic problems – a rather ridiculous idea – nor to provide a complete set of detailed policies. I am instead making some suggestions about what I believe would be a more helpful direction of travel. The financial crisis was and continues to be multi-dimensional. No single person or institution can solve the issues on their own. We need to become multi-disciplinary and co-operative in our approach to finding solutions. My purpose is to suggest some new ways in which we might imagine the nature and purpose of the investment markets and of large businesses. I invite you to contribute your experience and expertise.

TIME TO PRUNE – EVERYTHING

[2] Robert Burns *To a Mouse* 1785.

As every vine keeper knows, to produce good wine you must prune the vine every winter. The pruning process cuts away healthy growth, as well as growth that is old or diseased, in order to produce a better crop next season. Similarly, ploughing is a necessary process. A landscape that sought forever to be in harvest would soon be exhausted. Cutting through the toughened surface of the ground, turning over the stubble from last year's crop, and uncovering the fresh earth for a new planting is not a rejection of what has gone before. It is a vital preparation for a new season.

It may seem depressing that we are at the beginning of perhaps a decade of zero growth. At least a short winter must, however, be allowed to follow on from what has been an extended autumn of reaping. We should use the current season well as we consider how next to plant. We should not let a sense of regret about the past, let alone a sense of fear about the future, stop us from asking some deep questions about the world of finance and business. We need to be honest enough to admit that some things need to change, and courageous enough to turn to some new solutions.

Our finance reflects our philosophy. Western business and finance are the products of the Western culture from which they have grown. If we want to change business and finance we as a society need to change the way we think. We have done it before: the Reformation of the 16th century and the Enlightenment of the 18th century. No lesser change is needed now. Action follows thought.

Our thinking has altered considerably since the days of Adam Smith. We have become more individualistic, more reductionist, more utilitarian, more fearful, more disparate, more arrogant and more pragmatic. And so has business and finance.

We have become individualistic because our focus on the individual has morphed into a belief that the interests of all are best served if we each pursue our own interests. According to this logic, there is no need to seek the welfare of others because the welfare of others is best served if I serve only my own interests.

The scientific method has developed into a creed that dividing complex problems into their constituent elements is the best way to analyse them. This reductionist outlook has diminished our understanding of systems. Systems can only be understood by examining the relationships between actors since the relationships matter as much as the actors.

These individualistic and reductionist beliefs have blinkered us as to the consequences of our actions on others. We are no longer trained to think about the effects of our actions. We mistakenly assume that we are forever immune from the impact of our behaviour on the society and the environment in which we live, and our levels of concern for others has diminished accordingly.

Just as economics has come to dominate all policy decisions so utilitarianism, the belief system of economics, has come to dominate our moral imaginations. Economics claims to be an amoral space where what matters most is putting scarce resources to best use. In doing so it has inverted the proper order of things, turning individuals into subjects who can serve financial utility, rather than continuing to see them as the objects which financial utility is intended to serve. The value of others has been diminished to one of usefulness to us.

We naturally fear for provision and protection. Living alongside others, however, who have become increasingly individualistic, reductionist and utilitarian has, not surprisingly, increased these fears. We are responding by rejecting trust and seeking to control both others and our futures, whereas we should be developing a skill set that equips us with an appetitive for adventure to respond to the inevitably chaotic and unpredictable nature of both individuals and events.

Our attachment to freedom of choice has left us unable to agree on a common destination. As a result we have lost the Aristotelian and Judeo/Christian understanding of development towards personal and societal fulfilment. Our rightful fear of judgementalism has left us unwilling to discern between what is helpful and harmful on that journey of development. And we have become obsessed about doing our own thing. Our disparate objectives make a common goal very difficult to identify, let alone to achieve.

Our technical progress has made us over confident. We have made the mistake of transposing to economic and social theory the certainties of science. We believed the efficient market hypothesis. We thought that by creating more financial activity we were creating a more perfect market, and we thought that a more perfect market would produce more beneficial outcomes for human wellbeing.

Our disquiet over notions of right and wrong, our increasing lack of trust, and our belief that policies must be evidence based, has left us unwilling to believe that universal principles are a sound basis for good decision making. We no longer trust that, on average and over the long-term, positive results flow from making decisions based on positive principles. This is not to argue against evidence based decision making. It is to argue that we need more humility about our supposedly scientific looking facts and conclusions, at least in economic and social theory. In the space created by that humility, if not beyond, lies the room for principle based decision making. After all, a commitment to human dignity does not find its source in the cold logic of evidence.

> *"Those rules of old discovered, not devised*
> *Are Nature still, but Nature methodized."* [3]

Business and finance, including the debt and equity capital markets, have come to reflect these trends in many ways. I believe we need to reverse them philosophically and practically. The supposed 'science' of economics and investment has in recent years failed us, and the current uncertainties place us in uncharted waters where the navigation tools we have become accustomed to are not up to the task. Perhaps more than at any time in recent history we need sound principles to guide us forward.

[3] Alexander Pope *An Essay on Criticism* 1711.

We are suffering from a crisis of purpose and consequence. We neither agree what it is we are trying to build nor do we understand the multi-faceted ways in which everything is connected. This has affected us personally and institutionally. In the words of Ian Hislop, the editor of the satirical magazine *Private Eye*:

> *"Maybe society gets the bankers it deserves. Somehow we accepted that greed was good, and that probity, conscience, philanthropy and do-gooding were boring, old fashioned Victorian values. Perhaps we were wrong."* [4]

It is not surprising that the cultural structures through which we operate have come to reflect our mistakes in no lesser way than we have ourselves. We have companies that are legally required to pursue their own interests and that are financially incentivised to externalise all damaging consequences. We have markets that operate as if the real economy on which they depend did not matter. We have a debt minded economy that is increasingly reducing economic relationships down to an ever increasing spiral of legal claims against others and away from notions of contribution and shared endeavour. We have an investment industry that seeks to extract maximum returns rather assist with the productive deployment of capital. We have savers and pensioners who do not consider the environmental or social implications of their investment decisions.

It follows that if we are to reshape the business and financial landscape then the primary task is to reshape the way in which we think. We need to move away from individualistic towards relational, away from reductionist towards holistic, and away from utilitarian towards neighbourliness. We need to move away from control towards adventure, and away from disparate towards purposeful. We need to move away from arrogant towards humility, and away from pragmatism towards principle. The suggestions made in this book are designed to help us achieve this.

When the financial crisis first hit us there was no end of technical reasons being given as to why it had happened. Trade imbalances, regulatory failings, inadequate financial models, and so on. Only one human failing contributed, so it was said: the greed of bankers. This seemed to me to vastly short change the depth and complexity of the human issues involved, both inside and outside the City. So I was delighted when the debate moved on to 'cultures and behaviours'; a recognition that there was a broader malaise.

However, these two debates remain in isolated and unconnected pockets. We need to connect them. Technical fixes are being worked on in one corner. Cultures and behaviours are being worked on in another. What needs to happen, but has not happened yet, is an appreciation of the feedback loops between, on the one hand, the infrastructure of business and finance and, on the other hand, the cultures of which they are a part.

---

[4] Ian Hislop *When Bankers were Good* BBC 22 November 2011.

Positive values help to create positive institutions, and positive institutions help to foster positive values. Sadly, it is also true that negative values help to create negative institutions, and that negative institutions help to foster negative values.

Some want to go back to business as usual; the same financial architecture, just slightly nicer people running the show. I do not believe that can or will happen. Instead, I believe we need our positive values to mould the very nature of our business and financial institutions. If we do not then the strength of their business models and products will continue to overwhelm both those who work for them and the rest of us. If the work being done in the City on cultures and behaviours does not change the way in which the finance industry does business then it will have failed. The restoration of trust that the City seeks will only come about as the City demonstrates that it is worthy of trust by the actions it takes in response to the financial crisis.

Lionel Barber, editor of the *Financial Times*, commented in March 2012 that:

> *"There is a widely held view, whether mistaken or not, that political leaders have not been bold enough in reforming business practice and the regulatory system for banking and financial services."* [5]

I believe that four bold steps are now needed. Each of them is designed to help business and finance become more relational, more holistic, more neighbourly, more adventurous, more purposeful, more humble and more principled. Each of them is designed to help the architecture of business and finance reflect the positive values to which we aspire and in turn make it easier for us as individuals to continue to hold and to implement those positive values in practice.

START HERE

JOSH'12

[5] Lionel Barber *Boldness in Business* 21 March 2012.

The steps are these:

- to refocus mega-businesses, those businesses that control the way in which we live, by giving them a public responsibility as well as a private purpose,

- to reduce significantly and permanently the level of personal, corporate and national debt,

- to discourage speculation and financial transactions divorced from the real economy that consist merely of rights to claim against others, and

- to realign the investment markets so that they are looking to deploy capital for productive use as well as for a financial return.

Mega-businesses are here to stay, but their current objectives in too many cases are too separated from the wellbeing of the society of which they form part. They need to be refocused so that the benefits they undoubtedly bring to many of us are not incidental to their operations but are core to their purpose. This will produce social and environmental benefits for everyone. It will also increase, in the long run, their financial benefit for investors. And it will release the creativity of their employees, many of whom are currently uninspired by cultures that focus purely on the bottom line.

Excessive debt produces inflation, injustice and the modern day equivalent of slavery, where the economic futures of men and women are committed to a debt they cannot repay. Excessive debt centralises power, fuels speculation and turns others into a means not an end. The current economic climate can leave us in no doubt that we need substantially less debt. Government reforms to date might or might not make banks safer. They have done little, however, to address the quantum of debt. Reducing the level of personal, corporate and national debt will make our personal, corporate and national finances more stable, more equitable, more sustainable, and more enjoyable. Austerity or more debt are not the only two alternatives, as we shall explore.

Speculative trading is problematic partly because there is no sense of responsibility for any underlying business or the economy as a whole, and if you are not responsible you are unlikely to care. Similarly, claims-based trading, hedging arrangements that in return for a price allow us to make financial claims on others that do not vary depending on their future profitability, has produced a financial climate in which too many are uninterested in the welfare of the society or the business that produces those profits. Together, speculative and claims-based trading have begun to be destructive to the process of efficient capital allocation. The market was not designed to be used for these purposes on this scale.

As regards more productive investment, many have remarked that we need more of a stewardship economy, where owners of capital exercise husbandry over the companies in which they are invested. Stewardship, however, is about more than the use of voting rights after the investment decision has been made. It is also about where we decide to invest in the first place. Every economic decision is a social decision because every economic decision has a consequence for others.

Every individual has a responsibility to others as well as to self when choosing where to invest. And what is true for individual investors is just as true for institutional investors. We have a responsibility to put our capital to productive use. This is not to deny that we can and should seek a reasonable financial return. It is to suggest that we can and should also factor social and environmental consequences into our decision making processes, and not least because they impact long term financial sustainability. This is not a call to focus on avoiding the negative. It is a call to focus on seeking the positive. After all, as investors we can benefit not only from our positive financial returns but also from the positive society that the companies in which we invest can create. There is no conflict between financial and social usefulness. In fact, they are mutually reinforcing.

I refer to this kind of investing as 'bi-productive investing'. Modern investment has mostly become a mathematical exercise where the investor seeks to maximise its financial return commensurate with risk. It is largely uninterested in where or how money is invested. Bi-productive investment, by contrast, intentionally seeks to be productive twice – for the investor at one end of the investment chain, and for the company and its other stakeholders at the other end.

I believe that, together, these four suggestions would radically improve the business and financial environment in which we live. Together, they would create a more constructive, more just and more humane society. They would reconnect responsibilities with rights, but not in a way that is burdensome or overly restrictive. They would free us to be more intentional about being positive. They would restore both the reputation and the capacity of the market economy; the most effective tool yet invented by humankind, when suitably channelled, for economic advancement, wealth creation and the improvement of wellbeing. In the process we would hopefully rediscover that goodness is not simply good in an abstract sense; it is also good because it brings good things to pass for us and for others.

We also need to find a new way of practicing economics. Economics has disappointed us for numerous reasons. In part this has been our own fault because we have known about various market failures and inefficiencies but decided not to address them; issues such as growing monopolies, asymmetric information and conflicts of interest. And we have also chosen to allow economic considerations to crowd out all of the other things that we as individuals and society value. Economics has also disappointed us because some of its theories, as practiced over the last few decades, have simply been wrong, including the efficient market hypothesis. The fact that, unlike in other sciences such as chemistry, leading economists disagree with each other so strongly should have alerted us to the need to be more circumspect about endorsing modern economic theories so wholeheartedly. Economics, at least as currently constructed and taught, will always fail us whilst it continues with its quest to map with certainty the future decisions of individuals. This is not to deny the benefits of behavioural economics. It is to sound a warning bell for the hubris that may follow from attempting, and particularly for economic reasons, to map the future of humanity. It is not just that humans make perfectly valid, if 'irrational', choices for reasons of art, altruism or deliberate awkwardness. It is also that no human theory can capture the potential of humanity to create something out of nothing, love the unlovable or choose freedom over predictability. Such a theory would be attempting to deny humanity itself.

We now need a new breed of economics; one that is pneumatically filled by positive values and shared goals.

Some argue that the investment markets are now so fraught with problems that no one should invest. But battles are not won by removing oneself from the field of conflict. Nor are battles won only by force of arms. Battles are also won by influencing the belief systems of those who have a different perspective.

> *"I have found that if you want to make slow, incremental improvement, change your attitude or behaviour. But if you want to improve in major ways – I mean dramatic, revolutionary, transforming ways – if you want to make quantum improvements, either as an individual or as an organisation, change your frame of reference. Change how you see the world, how you view management and leadership. Change your paradigm, your scheme for understanding and explaining certain aspects of reality. The great breakthroughs are breaks with old ways of thinking."* [6]

Mine is not an anti-business agenda. Far from it. When business and finance perform their role in society well they make a contribution to the wellbeing of mankind that no other public or private actor in society can make. Business, well served by finance and well regulated by government, can enable all sectors of society to flourish, provide goods and services for customers, meaningful work for individuals and their families, and a reasonable return for investors. Business and finance so crafted can help communities benefit from their natural and intellectual resources, promote positive behaviours, and increase cooperation within and across national boundaries.

In any event, our problems do not arise solely as a result of finance in particular or business in general. The banking crisis has revealed a deeper and more political crisis. Current generations of Western politicians and voters are responsible for the welfare promises they have made to each other, and the cost of the public services they have created, that cannot be met without seriously encumbering future generations.

[6] Stephen R. Covey *Principle-Centred Leadership* 1990.

2. Mega-businesses: private gain and public duty

The birth of the mega-business

So we need business, and the trade that sits alongside it. The wealth created by business reduces poverty, stimulates innovation, and increases the demand for the rule of law. There is a strong connection between economic development on the one hand and democracy and peace on the other.

Over the last few decades, however, we have seen some businesses take on a different and more dominant nature. Many are now of a size and complexity unimagined by previous generations, and they have an influence on private lives, smaller enterprises, public affairs and international relationships that might amaze our forefathers.

The huge benefits brought about by globalisation are clear. There are, however, many reasons to think that business that is big is not necessarily business that is bright, and it is my belief that mega-businesses now need to be given a new sense of direction – a direction that has more of an explicit societal purpose and less of a self-orientated reason for existence. In terms of human history, the mega-businesses that now span the globe are very new kids on the block. Society has little experience of reacting to the changed relationships that they represent.

The term 'mega-businesses' is intended to mean any enterprise that has a significant impact on a community in which it operates or which it serves, whether that is in terms of employment, sourcing, supply or environmental impact. Many but by no means all mega-businesses are listed multinationals. Some mega-businesses are state owned or privately held businesses. The key is whether they are exerting in a particular area of life a significant influence over the way in which we live, either on their own or along with a small number of other similar large businesses. To be an enthusiast for business and an enterprise economy is not necessarily to support the mega-business on an unconditional basis.

In March 2012 Deutsche Bank sponsored a conference in Frankfurt entitled 'A New Deal – Balancing Corporate and Public Needs.' This puts the challenge neatly. It is time, I believe, to reset the social contract that exists between mega-businesses and society.

Externalities and cost

Mega-businesses are normally constituted as companies, and the law relating to their constitution is remarkably consistent around the world. They share a number of common themes, including a constitution or legal framework that requires the company, or its managers, to pursue the financial success of the company. This is the key to understanding both the problem of mega-businesses and the solution.

The pursuit of financial success causes a mega-business (and indeed any for-profit company) to seek to maximise profit, by minimising and externalising both cost and risk as much as it can. This process of externalisation is in many cases obvious and, because our society attaches particular significance to measures of an economic nature, those externalities that can be priced mathematically seem to carry particular weight. So I will give one such example.

In the 48 years after 1950 it is estimated that the externalities of China's substantial deforestation, to serve its construction and other industries, amounted to around US$12 billion, every year[7]. Those costs were incurred through the subsequent loss of watershed protection, soil erosion, flooding and droughts. The costs were not borne by the businesses that had caused the deforestation, but by others along river basins subsequently devastated by the consequences.

The difficulties in assessing, quantifying and costing externalities are significant, particularly if one is looking for standard measures for doing so. We should not, however, make the mistake of valuing only that which can be measured from an economic perspective, any more than we should be constrained by a need to establish an economic justification in order to preserve the wellbeing of individuals.

Issues around causation and the philosophy of value are also numerous when considering externalities. The difficulties are compounded because the externalities are often incurred on the other side of national boundaries. Depleted fish stocks, financial losses, environmental pollution, and water loss know no national boundaries. This gives rise to geo-political problems of appropriate cost and risk allocation. These difficulties do not, however, mean that the issues do not matter.

MARVELOUS ROOF!   NICE KITCHEN!

JOSH'12

---

[7] TEEB *The Economic of Ecosystems and Biodiversity Report for Business – Executive Summary* 2010.

The externalities of size

There are, however, many less obvious ways in which businesses externalise cost and risk, and these become more significant for society as an enterprise becomes a mega-business.

The banking crisis has shown us, for example, that individual banks have little regard for systemic risk. This is partly because our reductionist education equips us poorly to identify or understand systemic risk. Indeed, the implications of complex dynamic systems play almost no part in the modelling of financial risk, which relies on predictability, complete information, rational decisions and historic evidence. Behaviour within systems, however, is chaotic, complex and unpredictable. 'Banking pollution' describes the damaging effects on society of a poorly structured and over leveraged banking sector that did not take account of systemic risk. Under whatever measure one might choose to adopt, the pollution externalised by banks in recent years has been colossal.

Companies are also increasingly operating at the edge of their competencies as a result of competitive pressures and investor expectations. This seems to have been the case with BP's Deepwater Horizon, but it is also the case among banks, insurance companies and financial investors trading in securities they may not fully understand. The investment in research and development of new technology for products and services, including financial ones, is increasingly out of balance with the investment devoted to risk identification, prevention and remediation. There was, for example, significant underinvestment by the banks in the infrastructure necessary to understand and manage the sub-prime products they held on their balance sheets. And when a large player in a market makes a competency mistake the risk to society is increased because the consequences of that mistake tend to reverberate louder and further.

In the name of efficiency, there has also been a significant change in recent years in the trade-off between business stability and financial efficiency. Many businesses now carry minimal stock, outsource vital functions to third parties they cannot control, rely on suppliers without giving them support, and leverage their operations with significant debt. In other words, businesses are taking greater risks with less inbuilt operational resilience; and others are frequently feeling the consequences when the business stumbles or falls. The consequences are amplified when the business is big.

Economies of scale are usually claimed as the key benefit sought when mega-businesses acquire other companies. However, with an increase in size comes an increase in the costs of control and these may soon come to cancel out any efficiencies obtained. The following is the view expressed in March 2010 by Andrew Haldane, Executive Director Financial Stability, Bank of England:

> *"There is no strong evidence of increased bank efficiency after a merger or acquisition. And there is little evidence to suggest cross-activity mergers create economic value."*

Scale also reduces the resilience of society in another respect. Companies tend to have command and control mentalities. This means that, even after a period of reflection, they tend to take one-way bets with their strategic decisions. Their inclination is to develop a single house view, and then follow it closely. And given the human tendency to believe and follow conventional wisdom this makes them, and therefore the rest of the economy, less resilient to life's uncertainties than would otherwise be the case. Monopolies do not only reduce competition; they also reduce the benefits of strategic diversity. As we have seen in the banking sector, when a market is dominated by a relatively small number of very large players the risk to society of a systemic problem within that market is increased because there is no other harbour in which to weather the storm. Diversification by mega-businesses, including full service banks, does not avoid systemic risk if all of those businesses are diversifying in the same way. Diversity of business model, a different concept entirely, is more beneficial to society. Complex and diverse is more resilient than complex and similar.

It is not only banks that are too large to fail. This is dangerous where mega-businesses have, through a combination of investor inertia and their legal constitutions, become effectively unaccountable either to the market or to the societies in which they operate.

Large companies tend to be effective lobbyists. Although the connections between large companies and government are stronger in the US than in the UK, our own mega-businesses have a strong voice in shaping government policy. In many smaller jurisdictions their influence is even more powerful. This lobbying is, as one might expect, mostly in the interests of business, and policy makers often find it difficult to gainsay it.

> *"The knowledge that large financial services companies have direct and strong political connections, and use them, has been <u>and continues to be</u> a significant influence on regulatory action."* [8] (My emphasis)

It is usually more difficult to argue the case for the long-term social and economic benefits of prudence, because of problems of uncertainty and quantification, than it is to argue the case for the short-term benefits of particular business measures, particularly when those short-term benefits appear to favour a number of stakeholders, and not just business.

Mega-businesses do bring benefits, and that is why they make profits. Profits are a strong test of their social usefulness. If customers do not find a firm's products or services useful then they will not buy them. That simple formulation, however, is too simplistic in an environment where there are limited alternatives or where, for example, the products or services have an advertising budget behind them that overwhelms the imaginations of customers. Some responsibility for producing and selling goods and services that are of genuine benefit to customers must remain with the business, and therefore indirectly with its shareholders.

[8] John Kay *Narrow Banking, The Reform of Banking Regulation* 2009

The issue is not one of abuse of a dominant market position. It is one of concern about the extent to which mega-businesses control the way in which we live without needing to accept the public responsibility that comes with that power. There are numerous examples; a small number of supermarkets controlling the way we eat; Glencore controlling the trade in a number of metals; Rio Tinto, BHP Billiton and Vale Group dominating iron ore extraction; RBS, Lloyds, HSBC and Barclays controlling the UK small to medium sized lending market; a small number of companies controlling agricultural commodities; Google controlling the way in which we search for information; a few companies controlling cloud computing; a small number of companies that supply mobile phone services; two companies that dominate the supply of personal computing.

Competition law

It might be thought that effective competition law would prevent mega-businesses from gaining the kind of market power that gives rise to these types of concern. Competition law has not, however, been designed with this end in mind. It is not even clear that it should be, since we do benefit from the ability to invest and ability to compete on a global basis that mega-businesses can bring. The problem lies more in the purposes to which this kind of power is put.

Competition law does not generally stop a mega-business from building a controlling position in any particular market, unless that position is built through a merger or acquisition. Mergers that may harm competition and result in, for example, higher prices, reduced quality or choice for consumers, or reduced innovation may or may not be reviewed and prevented by the appropriate regulators. Competition law does not, however, prevent a mega-business from gaining control of a market, either on its own or with others, through organic growth, including through the use of exclusive intellectual property rights. It simply prevents the mega-business from abusing that position, and abuse is a strong concept.

Where competition law as applied in the UK might be more directly criticised is in the area of mergers. When mega-businesses combine generally either the European or the UK competition authorities, usually not both, review the merger. In recent years there has been a belief that Europe needs to build large business champions who can compete on an international scale. If the merger is large, it is generally the European authorities that conduct the review, and they consider the combination by reference to competition on an EU-wide basis not a national basis. The result is that mergers of mega-businesses can be approved that may not have serious adverse effects on competition in the European Union but may do in the UK.

Furthermore, competition law does not seek to address the externality risks to society mentioned above, such as systemic risk, competency risk, business reliance risk, financial risk, diversity risk or political influence risk. Nor does it measure the lack of choice available to consumers in a market controlled but not 'abused' by a dominant player. Nor does it impose on the mega-business any obligation to use its market power positively in the interests of customers or society. For an economist, the opposite of competition is not cooperation but monopoly. I am suggesting that the antidote to control is not necessarily more competition; it can also be civic duty.

The current Brussels competition review of Google is a case in point. It is examining whether Google abuses its position by giving unfair preference to its own services or by manipulating the results of searches to harm its rivals. It is not examining the extent to which it is in the public interest for just one company to control the way in which much of the world finds information. I am not suggesting that this near monopoly be removed from Google. I am suggesting that it would be preferable if Google accepted an appropriate degree of responsibility for acting in the public interest. Google has said that it wants to re-write what it means to be a good corporate citizen in the 21st century with its 'do no evil' strap line and its Google Ideas platform. Given the level of control it exercises over so many aspects of the way in which we live, the public needs to be assured that it, and others like it, will be as good as its word.

Private purpose

It can be argued that all of the externalities that mega-businesses export, and the degree of control that they exercise over the way in which we live, are a price worth paying in return for the benefits that they can bring. Sadly, customers seem only too pleased in many instances to see companies externalise costs and risks on their behalf, in order to lower consumer prices, turning a blind eye to the effects of them doing so on others. There is, however, a growing voice that both rejects this argument and wants to see mega-businesses use their power for public benefit not just private purpose.

The problems are in no small measure due to a particular difficulty that is inherent within virtually all companies. Whilst for decades the consequences of this difficulty lived within acceptable boundaries, in recent years they have become, in my view, too significant to go on accepting. The difficulty lies, as mentioned above, in the legally required purpose of companies.

Imagine that you live next door to a neighbour who is pathologically incapable of being anything but selfish. The neighbour is no fool, however. He realises that he cannot consistently and continually exploit his relationship with you because on occasion he needs you. You would, I suggest, not welcome such a neighbour. Or imagine that you live in a nation ruled by a dictator. Some would argue that a dictator can bring stability and order. But this dictator is not benign. He has not taken an oath to serve his people. He has considerable power and he uses it for the benefit of himself and his backers. He taxes his subjects heavily, although he is canny enough to realise that it is not in his interests to exhaust their resources.

Neither of these is a happy scenario, and yet the management of most for-profit companies believe with some justification that they are required to think and to act along these lines. Companies are indeed required by their constitutions to be self-centred. Once upon a time this may not have mattered, but it does matter in a world where globalisation has put some businesses on steroids.

Take the requirements of UK law as an example. It requires directors to promote, and only to promote, the success of their company for the benefit of their shareholders. This is interpreted as meaning financial success. This is equivalent to living alongside a large neighbour who is not only pathologically selfish but legally required to be so.

It is true that the UK Companies Act 2006 introduced for the first time an additional requirement for directors to 'have regard' to a number of other social and environmental factors. This so-called 'enlightened shareholder' model in theory puts UK law ahead of the law in many other nations. In practice, however, very little has changed. This is for two reasons.

First, the phrase 'have regard' carries so little weight. I can satisfy the requirement to 'have regard' to the victims of a car crash simply by looking at them as I drive by. There is little evidence that the requirement to 'have regard' has altered the outcome of board decisions in any meaningful way. And in most jurisdictions even this nod in the direction of other considerations does not exist.

Second, little has changed because even when I do notice the victims of the crash neither the law relating to directors' duties nor the statutorily required purpose of the company offers any basis upon which to prefer the interests of those victims over my own need to get to my destination. The law instead encourages an amoral, utilitarian attitude towards society and the environment. The law implies that although one may 'have regard' to the interests of a company's actions on employees, suppliers and customers, one may only do so in so far as those implications affect the long-term success of the company. That is self-centredness defined.

Public purpose

Many mega-businesses appear to have lost their sense of public purpose. It can no longer be assumed that an invisible hand creates socially beneficial outcomes from the capitalist who intends only his own benefit. Even if that was true in 1776 when Adam Smith wrote *The Wealth of Nations* it is no longer true when the capitalist considers himself free of moral considerations other than those imposed by law and when the society to which he might owe allegiance is an unidentified international community rather than his own national or local community. Adam Smith's *Theory of Moral Sentiments*, in which he had highlighted that virtue was an indispensable foundation for a market economy, preceded *The Wealth of Nations*. He would have been amazed at the idea that the invisible hand would have produced a socially beneficial outcome if companies that behaved like the British East India Company in 1776 conducted all business.

Pursuing one's own interests might have worked for the benefit of all in a society that pursued that end within a framework that had a sense of duty that was as strong, if not stronger, than its sense of entitlement. It does not work in today's environment. There is no invisible hand if civic responsibility is forgotten.

It is not too much to expect that a tyre manufacturer will be concerned about the safety of its customers, even if they know nothing about compounds and pressures and regulators have not prescribed for every eventuality. It is not too much to expect that a fashion retailer will be concerned about conditions in its Far Eastern supply chain, even if customers are not demanding a living wage for them and local legal requirements are inadequate. It is not too much to expect that a pharmaceutical company will not acquire the intellectual property rights to a new drug that cures a debilitating disease in order to prevent its production and preserve the market share of its own profitable but merely palliative treatment.

Nor do free markets necessarily produce good social results. It is, for example, clear that the offshoring of capacity by US mega-businesses is putting the fabric of some parts of US society under serious pressure. This may in turn threaten the mega-businesses themselves as their domestic market comes under pressure. The same may increasingly become the case in the UK. It is also clear that the market on its own may fail to address, within the necessary timeframe, the required transition to a lower carbon economy.

In previous decades UK companies were required to state their objectives at the beginning of their constitution. Whether that was to make biscuits, mend shoes or build houses they knew what their contribution to the fabric of society was meant to be. They defined, in effect, something of their public purpose. No constitution said that their objective was simply to make money. It was instead assumed that profits would follow according to the law of obliquity through pursuing a customer focused agenda by selling quality goods and services at reasonable prices. Case law and statute eroded the concept of clearly stated objectives, and to all intents and purposes the concept has now disappeared.

We may be able to continue to live alongside small or medium sized companies that remain firmly focused on pursuing their own interests. But for mega-businesses, the rules of the game should in my view now be changed.

The price for limited liability

Mega-businesses need to be encouraged to think and behave more like responsible individuals within a family, aware of the benefits of pursuing their own interests but also seeking the welfare of the society of which they are part. Under the normal rules of social behaviour one is required to accept responsibility for the consequences of one's actions. We may have 'limited liability companies', where the liability of the shareholders as owners of the business is limited to the capital they have invested, but there is no such thing as limited liability. There is only liability allocation. Liabilities do not magically evaporate when a business becomes insolvent. They are left to be borne by others. The shareholders of mega-businesses should accept that the companies in which they invest must carry an element of public responsibility as the price for being granted by society immunity from responsibility through the gift of limited liability. Rights divorced from responsibilities usually cause problems.

Some have taken the view that through the process of institutional investors encouraging companies to focus on the environmental, social and governance (ESG) agenda the same result will be achieved. But I believe this will prove ineffective because this approach does not respond to the underlying problem of corporate selfishness. The ESG agenda is based on the premise that, in the long-term, no sensible company would want to damage the society in which it operates because it depends on that society. But this ignores the short to medium term benefits to a company of leaving to other members of society the cost of remedying the consequences of its actions. What is missing from ESG, including the corporate governance agenda, is any inspiration to act positively for the benefit of society. It is encouraging perhaps that the signatories to the UN Principles of Responsible Investment represent over US$25 trillion in assets under management. It is telling, however, that investors with so much firepower have, to date, not managed to change the mantra of so many mega-businesses. The logjam is, I believe, the corporate purpose of mega-businesses.

I am not suggesting that mega-businesses should take on responsibility for the welfare of society as a whole. I am suggesting that, within the particular spheres in which they operate, they should be encouraged to accept a measure of responsibility for the wellbeing and positive development of that sphere.

For example, whilst they retain their current level of size and influence, banks should accept a degree of responsibility for the financial welfare of their personal customers, for providing finance for business and for ensuring the stability of the financial system. This would include taking active steps to help individuals budget and save rather than borrow and spend. Supermarkets and food manufacturers should accept a measure of responsibility for the nutritional welfare of shoppers and the sustainability of national food production. The media should accept responsibility for truthful and responsible reporting. Mining companies should accept a measure of responsibility for environmental sustainability, community welfare and inter-generational fairness, and oil companies should accept a measure of responsibility fo working towards a lower carbon economy. And when operating in low income countries, both mining and oil companies should accept a measure of responsibility for enabling governments to build their governmental and developmental capacities and objectives.

Anti-capitalists attack the profit motive of big business. That is not the aim here. The profit motive that creates wealth remains a vital and valuable source of endeavour. It is just that we need neighbours who are siblings not ogres.

A company is only a construct of convenience of creative imaginations and legal propositions. It has no physical existence or actual substance. There is in reality no such thing as the separate legal personality that the law confers on companies. In reality there are only human beings, trading with each other, albeit at a distance. If we are to create legal propositions that institutionalise businesses and pretend they are people, let us have propositions that are less binary from a social perspective. Let us have propositions that do not grant mega-businesses immunity from the ordinary decencies of humanity that we would expect of people.

Introducing public duty

There are at least three possibilities for connecting mega-businesses with public duty.

It may be tempting to think first of giving the task to governments and regulators. That may be necessary, but it would be regrettable. It is the role of governments to create the conditions in which we can flourish, and preferably not to exercise choices that we are better off making for ourselves. Responsibilities are more willingly and enthusiastically endorsed and fulfilled if they are responsibilities that have been freely adopted.

One mechanism for allowing shareholders in UK mega-businesses to make this choice for themselves already exists. A seldom-used provision, section 172(2) of the Companies Act 2006, allows shareholders to introduce a more varied set of corporate objectives than merely their own financial benefit. It allows shareholders to decide on their own definition of success, and not merely in a way that separates financial and social objectives into competing goals.

The shareholders to ask are not the shareholders of record. Sadly, too many asset management businesses, hedge funds, pension trustees and insurance companies have to date shown too little interest in exercising even basic rights of stewardship over the companies in which they have invested their clients' money. The shareholders to ask are, instead, their clients: the individuals who are the ultimate end-owners of all capital and who are, of course, all members of society in other capacities as well; whether as employees, consumers, parents or simply citizens. Whether we as savers and pensioners have or would develop the presence of mind to make the right choices remains to be seen. To date no one has asked us. We will return to the issue of shareholder democratisation in Chapter 5.

It would be helpful if mega-businesses took the lead in formulating and putting forward to investors their proposed civic responsibilities. In doing so it would be important for their boards to consult widely with employees, who can often see with more clarity the positive impact potential of the business for which they work. Involvement in decision making of course also increases motivation, and a public recognition by a mega-business of its welfare responsibilities is likely to further encourage employees to give of their best given the increased sense of self-worth and satisfaction that comes from contributing towards a project that is focused on helping others.

Some bold mega-businesses are not waiting for permission to pursue this more positive agenda. Unilever, for example, launched a plan in 2010 with three goals: to help improve the health of more than a billion people, to halve the environmental footprint of its supply chain, and to source sustainably all of its agricultural raw materials. Wal-Mart, Marks & Spencer, GSK, Johnson & Johnson and Nestlé are all taking similar steps in some of their own fields, and it is noticeable that all of these companies have strong retail consumer connections. It is less clear whether business-to-business companies are moving in this direction. In any event, the need is to embed these changes, change investor expectations and spread their example to those others – the majority – who are less willing to follow suit, and to give assurance to the public that these changes are not a management fad but an entrenched change of tack.

If this voluntary approach proves insufficient there are two other alternatives.

One is to change the Companies Act definition of success for mega-businesses and provide for them instead an agenda that gives more prominence to the interests of all stakeholders. Instead of success being defined as the financial success of the company for the benefit of shareholders, mega-businesses could be required to return to defining their particular contribution to society (whether that be mining bauxite, growing corn, shipping fuel, or whatever). Success could then be defined as (a) the financial success of the company for the benefit of shareholders, together with (b) the promotion of the welfare of its other stakeholders, such as employees, customers, suppliers, the environment and the community, and (c) taking into account the public interest in relation to the promotion of the particular purpose of the company (mining bauxite, growing corn, shipping fuel) and the systemic, competency, business reliance, financial, diversity and political influence risks mentioned above.

A split supervisory and executive board might be an appropriate way in which to manage such mega-businesses. The supervisory board, with members representing the interests of stakeholders as described, would set guidelines to balance and blend various objectives. The executive board would be tasked with implementing those policies. A solution along these lines has the advantage of effectively internalising many of the costs of implementation and would therefore result in lower regulatory costs.

A second alternative is to expand the powers of government to enable it, through an appropriate agency, to require mega-businesses to promote the public interest in relation to their spheres of operation, and this may be necessary for mega-businesses operating in the UK that are not UK companies or that are not listed companies. This is not such a foreign concept as might first appear. Not surprisingly perhaps, the law already allows the government to intervene in business to protect against threats to national security. However, it also allows the government to intervene to protect against a narrow concentration of media or broadcasting that might restrict diversity and distort public opinion. And regulated utilities already have a public service responsibility. So some of the groundwork necessary for mega-businesses to accept an element of public responsibility through government intervention has already been done.

In all of these scenarios a more rounded form of corporate reporting would assist with clarifying the public purpose and monitoring the degree of fulfilment. Chapter 5 discusses moves to introduce reporting that covers not just financial but also social and other forms of capital and which would assist with this process.

For those mega-businesses unwilling to accept a measure of civic responsibility the answer is clear: demerge and give up control over the way in which we live.

3. Reducing excessive debt

The unstoppable logic of debt

It will not have escaped your notice that we have a problem with debt. What is strange, however, is how little discussion there has been about where this debt came from, what it has done to the way in which we live, and how we might go about preventing ourselves from falling into this trap again.

The bank reforms currently planned do not address this agenda. They may (in time) make banking safer, but otherwise they leave the financial realities of economic life relatively unchanged. The recent announcements by the Financial Policy Committee of the Bank of England (FPC) confirm the point. The FPC has made suggestions to HM Treasury as to the macro prudential policy tools it wishes to be granted, but the FPC still feels public support is insufficient to enable it to request powers to impose direct brakes on bank lending since this would directly restrict the amount that individuals and businesses could borrow. In other words the FPC has no plans to reduce debt, except in so far as that is the indirect consequence of trying to make banks safer.

Debt does have its advantages. It can be a convenient, simple and cheap method of allocating capital. It can enable a business to access finance without giving up control, and it can enable a business to receive funding in circumstances where an equity investment would not appropriate. Borrowing to finance working capital, and lending a small amount to help finance a venture that is risky, are two examples of where debt finance may be preferable to equity finance.

For individuals and corporates debt can enable us to manage our finances by bringing forward our expenditure and smoothing out our repayments over a longer period. It can similarly enable us to invest for increased productivity beyond the level of our savings. And, of course, the maturity transformation role that banks play, changing short-term deposits into long-term loans, is a valuable service to both savers and borrowers. The problem with debt, however, is as usual the second iced-bun not the first. It is excessive debt that is the problem.

The presence of large quantities of debt in our economy has deeply affected the way in which we think about economic relationships, and we have not yet learnt how to differentiate between helpful and excessive levels of debt. Let us first look, however, at the nature of debt and its connection with money.

Money is a social convention. Its existence is somewhat ethereal. It is clear that governments and banks can, and do, create money out of nothing simply by making the necessary book entries. What has been less well understood, however, is how money and debt have become opposite sides of the same coin in the modern economy (or more accurately, the opposite sides of the same computer entry). Debt and money are created together. [9] Martin Wolf, Chief Economic Editor of the *Financial Times*, has put it like this:

> *"The essence of the contemporary monetary system is the creation of money out of nothing, by bankers' often foolish lending."* [10]

Banks are, of course, incentivised to create as much money as possible (and therefore as much debt as possible) since by doing so they increase their capacity for making profits. Governments also seem unable to resist the temptation to issue debt, or to create new money through quantitative easing.

This kind of money is known as 'fiat money' because it was once created by government decree, although now it is mostly created by the decision of private sector banks (even if legally enforced by the government and in practice guaranteed by it as the bank bailouts have demonstrated). Dealing in the fiction that this kind of money is real, rather than simply a book entry, can be useful for a time. Problems emerge, however, when we take the myth too seriously. It is instructive that neo-classical economics led us into the crisis and that neo-classical economics does recognise debt in its models. Living with an unreality as if it were a truth is a dangerous strategy. Creating wealth is more complex than creating money.

CAN YOU PHOTOCOPY THIS £50 NOTE A MILLION TIMES PLEASE?

---

[9] For information on the creation of money out of nothing, and on the relationship between the creation of money and debt, see www.positivemoney.org.uk
[10] Martin Wolf *Financial Times* 9 November 2010.

We are currently in the middle of a particular manifestation of the problem of debt. The consequences of promises to pay that could not be met have first been absorbed by banks, then by governments, and now by supranational institutions. It is unclear what happens when confidence is lost in the ability of the International Monetary Fund or the European Central Bank to meet their promises. Private sector banks, central banks and governments are now caught in a potentially lethal embrace, with central banks paying private banks to acquire government debt.

Excessive debt produced a credit economy whose collapse was probably inevitable sooner or later. Its demise has led to an unsustainable, and highly centralised, central bank money economy; and certainly the most centralised economy that Europe has ever seen. The fear is that governments, central banks and a relatively small number of private sector banks are now seeking to manage the economy to stabilise each other rather than necessarily serve the public interest. It is entirely possible that the next transition will be uncomfortable. In the measured words of Thomas Mayer, Deutsche Bank's Chief Economist, the next change may be *"discontinuous"*.

Central bank support may have calmed liquidity concerns but it has not resolved the solvency issues. Only growth, or debt forgiveness, can do that, and at present growth is stuttering. There is no guarantee of a return to growth. There is a guarantee, absent debt forgiveness, of continuing interest charges and scheduled debt repayment dates. In fact it is in the interests of governments to engage quietly in a policy of financial repression, rather than either austerity or growth, by keeping the yield on government bonds slightly below inflation so that lenders receive back, in real terms, less than they lent.

Meanwhile, the tensions between creditor nations and their populations on the one hand, and debtor nations and their populations on the other, are only likely to grow. And, within debtor nations, distrust in politicians and civic institutions continues to mount. Excessive debt has entangled countries together in ways that the world has not previously needed to manage. It is not clear that we have the necessary political apparatus to manage the conflicts, nor the political will as citizens to make the kind of decisions that are necessary in the interests of others on such a cross-border basis. The government and bank debts, shadow banking connections and hedge fund strategies that now connect us have only relatively recently emerged. The world is poised to sue based on the contracts that represent debt. This is the unstoppable logic of debt in a world where we have not learnt to accept limits on its creation.

Government debt is no more than a promise made by the government to the bond markets to tax the citizens of tomorrow to meet the promises made by government to the tax payers of today. Politicians have not learnt how to put a cap on their welfare promises and are always tempted to kick the can of repayment down the road towards tomorrow. The government cannot issue equity, only debt. In a season when governments are anxious to fund themselves, some see more than a coincidence in the changing regulatory landscape that requires pension funds, insurance companies and banks to hold an increasing level of debt and in fiscal policies that maintain downward pressure on interest rates. However, one cannot get the better of the bond markets forever, and at some point the markets may decline to continue funding ever decreasing yields and ever decreasing sovereign credit qualities.

Lawrence Summers, the former US Treasury Secretary, sums up the current overriding objectives of governments:

"Government has no higher responsibility than insuring economies have an adequate level of demand. Without growing demand, there is no prospect of sustained growth, let alone a significant fall in joblessness. And without either of these there is no chance of reducing debt-to-income ratios."

How sad that our collective dreams have been reduced by the political and economic establishment down to a simple desire to see us consume in order to reduce debt-to-income ratios. The lack of choice that this agenda suggests denotes modern day slavery: work simply to pay debts. Excessive debt has imprisoned our paradigms and our possibilities.

Ancient wisdom

Put simply, the total sum of debts has become greater than the worth of what is pledged against it, whether in terms of assets or reliable future income. What a joy it would be if we could all start again with debt free balance sheets! If only we could be released from the financial whirlwind that now circles around our heads with such unpredictable and destructive effects on the earth below.

Many ancient cultures were for good reason suspicious of interest bearing debt, known as usury, and imposed a combination of moral opprobrium and sometimes legal prohibition on all interest bearing debt. [11] (Classically, usury does not mean excessive interest. It means any interest.) This suspicion lasted well into the 16th century in the Protestant part of Europe, and later still in Catholic regions, although it was circumvented or ignored by a number of Italian and other banking families. Of course without interest bearing debt our financial system would look very different, not least because of an absence of banks.

Our forefathers were cuter than we might have imagined. They recognised that debt had a tendency to enslave both economically and psychologically. Even before banks were creating money, and debt, on the current industrial scale, and even before debt based economies were fashionable because of the previous distaste for lending money with interest, our forefathers recognised that every now and then it was necessary to step in and cut the Gordian knot if poverty and slavery, including the sense of alienation and hopelessness to which they give rise, were not to become permanently institutionalised.

---

[11] One of the best descriptions of this is given by George Goyder (the father of Mark Goyder, one of the founders of Tomorrow's Company) in an appendix to his book *The Just Enterprise* 1987.

Many ancient cultures celebrated the appointment of new rulers by cancelling debts. In ancient Israel this was embedded as a regular requirement of economic life. Every seven years all debts were cancelled and all slaves were liberated. The application of justice and mercy lay behind this unusual but radical solution to the build up of debt and social entrapment, although it no doubt also led to more affordable and responsible lending practices in the meantime. Justice without mercy fails the test of justice, and mercy without justice also falls short. Justice requires that promises to pay be duly fulfilled. Mercy dictates that occasionally it is necessary for lenders to forgive borrowers.

It may be that, absent any realistic prospect of growth for a decade, if we want to avoid disorderly defaults by governments, with the consequent social chaos and political unrest that would then follow, we should consider now a massive programme of debt forgiveness. Not a programme to lend further money through central banks to buy more time, in the futile hope that ever more indebted governments will one day repay. Instead, a massive gift by creditor nations to debtors nations. A huge act of unconditional generosity that recognises the benefits that richer nations have gained from the euro, and their fault in helping to design a currency union that was economically flawed and, some would say, politically disingenuous. An act of solidarity with the citizens of poorer nations who have been badly let down by their political and business leaders.

Having done so, all parties would be older and wiser as they then considered how best to build a more sustainable political and financial European structure. All parties would then also have the opportunity to reflect on the dangers of debt, and the importance of designing a new financial system that could not in future be fuelled by excessive debt. A full economic and political union, that further centralises power, brought about through a shotgun marriage in the face of insolvency does not seem a sound basis upon which to build a stable Europe.

Simply cancelling debts in the modern economy would cause too much chaos; the insolvencies amongst those to whom the debts were owed, and amongst those to whom they in turn owed debts, would cause widespread problems. A further alternative, at least on a national basis, may be a variant on the quantitative easing (QE) theme. At present QE appears to be mostly boosting bank reserves without resolving wider problems. Instead QE could be used, and effectively without creating more debt, to give money directly to every private person in the country. This would be on condition that it was used to repay their debts, and that those receiving repayment (for example banks) in turn repaid their debts (for example to bondholders). Those with no debts would still receive the gift and, although not central to the scheme, they could be encouraged to spend that money in ways that boosted the economy; preferably through investing in businesses that create employment or are looking to increase productivity. A beneficial by-product would be the shrinking of bank balance sheets back towards their pre-credit boom size and, together with implementation of the policies discussed below for restructuring banks, this would help prevent them from repeating the mistakes of the past. It was a sleight of hand that produced money/debt. Maybe it will take another to reduce it.

The dangers of excessive debt

As has been more than amply demonstrated, excessive debt results in an inevitable transfer of wealth – and therefore of power – from poor to rich. Over time, it turns lenders into masters and borrowers into servants. Excessive debt centralises power, and centralising power is almost always a mistake. It is not just a question of the tendency to corrupt. It is a question of insensitivity to the legitimate needs and concerns of others. One of the world's leading evolutionary biologists, Robert Trivers, puts it thus in his book *Deceipt and Self-Deception*:

> *"…when a feeling of power is induced in people, they are less likely to take others' viewpoints and more likely to centre their thinking on themselves."*

It is no coincidence that we have seen four other forces at work as the volume of debt has mounted. First, remuneration packages in the City, and in the businesses financed by debt, have grown substantially. Second, the corporate profits that fund those levels of remuneration, and which might more appropriately be the target of complaint, have also grown substantially (although, in recent years, levels of remuneration have even become detached from this measure). Third, democratic power has moved away from governments and their citizens and towards banks and the bond markets, and it is both of these that the technocrat governments installed by the European Commission are, for perfectly respectable and understandable reasons, now trying to save.

And, fourth, there are numerous statistics that demonstrate the widening gap in incomes in the West and that not everyone shares the benefits of growth. As the OECD has put it in the case of the US, *"the wealthiest Americans have collected the bulk of the past three decades' income gains."* The picture is similar elsewhere. The technology revolution and global outsourcing, both of which mean less demand for Western jobs, have caused much of this. Much of it, however, has been the result of the debt enhanced growth that has boosted the scope and reach of banks and other businesses.

There are strong calls for a return to 'business as usual', including 'normal' growth. It is not clear that 'normal' is helpful when the benefits of normal are increasingly being channelled into fewer and fewer hands. Some measure of financial inequality is inevitable, and even desirable if it demonstrates that those individuals who work hard, cleverly and honestly are being rewarded for doing so. It is less desirable, however, if it demonstrates that an economic system has begun to centralise power and wealth in the hands of those who are already economically or politically powerful. Such a system is not attractive in the short-term and is unsustainable in the long-term. It will in the end, as a result of the 'elite' seeking to protect their position, produce either social unrest or the stifling of the innovation that might otherwise benefit society.

Even without these longer term effects, however, excessive debt increases economic instability, magnifying the booms and busts that seem to be an inevitable part of the cycle of capitalism. This instability is a storm that can be weathered by the rich but less easily by the poor. Debt transfers the risk of what is always an uncertain future onto the shoulders of the borrower.

Debt is inherently inflationary, again favouring those with assets but penalising those living on limited or fixed incomes. Debt feeds a desire for now and finances impatience. It fuels an unsatisfying spiral of anxiety and consumption, with consequent implications for pollution and natural resource use. It tempts us, individually and corporately, into growth that is not matched by maturity and gives us permission to live beyond our means. It leaves our children with the burden of paying for our excesses and makes possible profligate public finances.

The cost of excessive debt is reflected in numerous personal stories, many of them tragic. Outstanding personal debt in the UK stood at £1.456 trillion at the end of January 2012, comprising secured debt of £1.248 trillion and unsecured consumer credit debt of around £208 billion. It is estimated that every day in the UK 318 people are declared insolvent or bankrupt, 1,473 consumer County Court judgments are issued, for an average of £2,949 per judgment, 93 properties are repossessed, and 275 landlord possession orders are made. The Citizens Advice Bureaux in England and Wales deals with 8,652 new debt problems every working day. [12]

In the investment markets, debt encourages strategies that prioritise capital gains based on increased asset prices, without any increase in the productivity or utility of the underlying business. It therefore encourages the obtaining of a financial reward without necessarily contributing to real underlying growth. Debt finances the familiar since the familiar normally has an asset base that can be provided as security. It does not finance innovation since innovation offers little by way of security. In a knowledge and service economy such as ours this is a particular shortcoming.

Debt offers us the opportunity to increase our profits by a significant multiple, but for the same equity investment and, when combined with the structure of a limited liability company, provides us with a powerful tool to externalise our increased losses and privatise our increased gains. Debt is therefore the handmaiden of speculation, a theme to which we will return in Chapter 4, and not least because it enables a corporate investor to trade based on an asymmetric relationship between risk and reward.

I WENT BUST. THESE ARE YOURS NOW...

LIABILITIES

Josh12

[12] Figures and estimates from Credit Action, March 2012.

The disinterest of debt

Debt also has a further and more significant impact in terms of economic relationships, one that is manageable in a low debt economy but more serious in a high debt economy. With equity finance, the investor's return is dependent on two things. First, a beneficial economic environment for the business to operate in and, second, a business that succeeds in the long term. In fact the more beneficial the economic environment, and the more successful the business, the better the investor does. There is a 'fairness' that results from equity because equity shares both risk and reward. [13] The equity investor is therefore incentivised to care about, and if necessary stake steps to support, both the broader economic environment and the particular business. Furthermore, equity is perpetual and must, therefore, include a long-term view.

Debt is different. Debt insists on its pound of flesh in all circumstances. Debt, and particularly secured debt, has a fixed financial return and a fixed repayment date (at least in theory) and is therefore, by comparison with equity, relatively indifferent as to the economic environment or the success of the business, whether in the short or longer term. Debt is binary; it narrows relationships down to contracts rather than shared endeavour. Since it does not share business risk, at least not intentionally, debt does not foster mutually constructive, two-way relationships, based on track record, trust or common purpose. Clearly banks do sometimes lose money on loans, but nevertheless debt has a tendency to lead to disinterested finance and a lack of sympathy from lenders for borrowers. Furthermore, debt can be (and has been) used, particularly within the private equity industry, to finance premature and over generous equity distributions at the expense of the stability of a business and the long-term interest of its owners in its prosperity. A variety of property based operating businesses were orphaned in this way prior to the banking crisis.

There are pressing calls for equity investors to play a greater stewardship role, and particularly to encourage the companies in which they are invested to improve their environmental, social and governance performance; not simply because that is a good thing to do but because it produces more beneficial long-term outcomes for all stakeholders. And yet an increasing percentage of investment portfolios is represented by debt, in part because of increasing over anxiety about the higher risk inherent in equities and in part because of attempts to match predictable pension liabilities with predictable bond returns. Debt has little interest in stewardship.

Debt engines

The banking sector is the engine that manufactures debt. Banks promise their depositors and bondholders a combination of liquidity, returns and security. They assure us that we can have our money back when we want it and that, in the meantime, they will pay us an income and keep our money safe. This is a promise they cannot keep. One cannot have all three of those features simultaneously. It is said that trust is a vital component of banking. It would be more accurate to say that suspending disbelief is a vital component of banking, at least in its current form.

---

[13] English law invented a legal concept called 'equity' (meaning fairness rather than an investment in shares) in medieval times as a counter to the otherwise hard logic of the demands of a contract. The legal concept of equity seeks justice where otherwise the terms of a contract might fail to provide it.

Most banks in the UK remain too big to fail, and they will continue to be so for many years to come. But the situation may become in some respects worse, not better, when they have been reshaped and divided so that the government feels it can then allow them to fail as proposed by the Vickers Report on restructuring the UK banking sector.[14] Even when recapitalised and reorganised, retail and commercial banks will remain stable only for so long as they are not subject to entirely possible disturbance. The failure of one bank may no longer cause the failure of others, but that will be of little comfort to those who lose money in the bank that fails.

If, however, you believe that the political ramifications of allowing a UK retail bank to fail are such that no government would ever let that happen, then we will remain locked into a system in which the tax payer continues to subsidise private sector profits and there is an on-going market failure because the fear of insolvency has been removed from the system.

The separation of investment banking from retail and commercial banking, as proposed by the Vickers Report, will also leave the investment banking model essentially unchanged, even if less profitable because of higher regulatory capital requirements.

That pressure on profitability is, among other things, likely to spur the investment banks on in their promotion of the debt capital markets as an alternative to traditional bank lending, since the investment banks are the controllers of the bond issuance process and can earn fees accordingly. This is concerning for a number of reasons. First, because the bond market is crowding out traditional bank lending to corporates, and therefore in turn traditional bank lending to small and medium sized enterprises, the engine of most economic growth. Second, because the bond markets show even less interest in stewardship than traditional bank lending. And, third, because it is already the case that only 12 investment banks control 58 per cent by volume of the global bond issuance market.[15] They are positioning themselves such that only they have the necessary knowledge, international relationships and underwriting strength to act as bookrunners on major debt capital market issues. The control by an even smaller group of global banks of certain derivatives that commonly accompany bond issues is even stronger. An oligopoly is growing over one of the world's major sources of finance.

IT RUNS ON SUSPENDED DISBELIEF

BANK

JosHi2

---

[14] *Final Report of the Independent Commission on Banking* September 2011.
[15] According to Euroweek figures for 2011.

Similarly, the Vickers Report does not cure the many and varied conflicts of interest present in modern investment banking, and particularly the conflict inherent between trading with their own capital for their own account and providing advice and services to clients. The length of an investment bank disclaimer tells one something of the depth and breadth of the problem, but there are some conflicts that, as a moral and business matter if not a legal matter, cannot be cured by transparency. An analogy would be a firm of estate agents advising clients on buying and selling houses whilst at the same time managing a portfolio for their own account. One simply would not believe that they would handle the conflicts appropriately, Chinese Walls notwithstanding. Investment bankers, post the financial crisis, are talking in terms of becoming 'professionals' and 'fiduciaries'. Professionals and fiduciaries are, for good reason, not permitted to have such conflicts. Nor should investment banks.

Reshaping debt

As the old joke goes, when asked the best way to Dublin the answer is that it is best not to start from here. But it is helpful to know that Dublin is a wonderful city and that it is worth making the effort to reach it.

Clearly it is a significant task to reverse our addiction to debt. Much work is needed to map the journey, and a great deal of analysis and international cooperation would be required. But we would find that it was worth the effort.

I am not proposing that we eliminate debt. However, having lost faith in the fiat money system because of the profligacy in public finances that it both permits and encourages, and having seen that the debt habit is addictive and harmful for individuals, corporates and nations, it is time to imagine some other possibilities. What I am proposing is that we take steps to reduce substantially the volume of debt, that we decommission and put beyond use the machinery that produces it, and that we consider moving towards an asset based money regime.

Two of the most significant signposts along the way would likely include a more radical restructuring of banks than the one proposed by Vickers and an abolition of the favoured tax treatment currently given to debt. Vickers may separate investment banking from commercial and retail banking, but it neither cures instability nor prevents the creation of excessive debt. Vickers, and the work of the FPC, is focused on making banks safer. It is not focused on making the rest of us healthier.

One proposal for restructuring banks is given by Positive Money.[16] As they say themselves, this is not necessarily the only or even the best way to go about the restructuring, but their full reserve banking proposal does demonstrate that it is possible to imagine other credible alternatives. Under their proposal banks would no longer operate on the basis of the fractional reserve model that currently permits them to create money and debt almost without limit and to run a bank in a manner that is inherently lacking in stability. The Governor of the Bank of England gave a speech in 2010 reviewing the structure of banks, including the fractional reserve model. He commented as follows:

"Of all the many ways of organising banking, the worst is the one we have today."[17]

Instead, under the full reserve model, banks would operate two forms of account. First, a non-interest bearing current account for day-to-day operations, limited to a modest amount effectively guaranteed (as now) by the government. Second, a savings account run by the bank along the lines of a mutual fund, with liquidity gates and notice periods for withdrawals, and with the nominal amount of the onward investments made by the bank never exceeding the savings made. As part of this restructuring, the payment system run by the banks (a utility on which we all depend) would be isolated from any investment risk. The onward investments made by the banks would include most of the forms of credit that we are used to today, including overdrafts, credit cards and commercial loans. They would, however, be likely to include a greater proportion of equity investments. And, of course, they would not be creating ever increasing amounts of debt by inventing money. The key issue, however, is that solvency and liquidity risk would have been solved.

Whether or not banks are remodelled in this way, we could in any event impose the loan-to-value ratios and loan-to-income ratios on bank lending that the FPC currently seems too shy to recommend. These would be transparent ways of limiting credit fuelled bubbles in commercial and residential property, and in other financial assets.

And we could set limits on the size of the UK assets of UK banks as a proportion of the size of the UK economy, with firewalls between their UK and overseas operations. The assets of UK banks were nearly five times UK GDP in 2009, compared to an equivalent multiple of one times in the US and three times in Germany and France.[18] The Dodd-Frank Act has begun the process of limiting the size of US banks. We should do likewise.

The objective of these steps would not be to protect the banks from over exposure, or even from systemic risk to themselves, although these would be beneficial by-products. Their primary objective would instead be to protect the UK economy, and the individuals who live within the UK, from the negative consequences of excessive debt. The only people who benefited from the growth in the size of RBS pre-financial crisis were its own employees and short-term investors – certainly not the UK economy or long-term investors.

[16] See the joint submission made to Vickers by Positive Money, the New Economics Foundation and the University of Southampton, Centre for Sustainable Banking and Finance.
[17] Mervyn King *Banking: From Bagehot to Basel, and Back Again* 25 October 2010.
[18] *Final Report of the Independent Commission on Banking* September 2011.

The right to create money, known as seigniorage, could also be removed from private sector banks and reserved for the government or a central bank office. It has been estimated that seigniorage revenues foregone are currently costing UK taxpayers £47 billion a year, and represent a £21 billion a year subsidy to UK bank profits. [19] The point of the reform is not, however, just to remove this unfairness but to return to democratic control the key policy tool of the amount of money/debt created in the economy.

Too big to live

We could also take steps to limit the ability of banks to externalise risk to others, which they currently achieve, for example, through the use of securitisations and derivatives. This limitation may have the effect of increasing the price of credit, but the unrealistically cheap price of credit, because of the previous under-pricing of risk, was an important contributor to the financial crisis and the subsequent externalising of significant losses by the banks. This shifted to taxpayers a cost that should have been borne in the first place by the original borrowers in terms of higher credit charges.

Banking is an unusual business. There is an inevitable instability about its business model. It is in the interests of banks to externalise that instability, and the sector is unusual in having created or supported numerous products that seek to do just that. JPMorgan Chase may have suffered embarrassing losses as it sought to externalise the risk of the US economy. But the real concern is not the losses, but the attempt itself. The episode illustrates the level of sophistication and comprehensiveness that this process of externalisation by banks of their own instability to the rest of the economy has now reached, and not just at JPMorgan Chase. It may be fine for banks to seek to defy the laws of gravity by desiring a profit through taking no risk. It is not fine when that comes at the price of asking the rest of the economy to assume those risks. No other industry behaves quite like this. Not just too big to fail. Too big to live.

Further remodelling

We could also require banks to take more stringent and responsible steps to ensure that individual borrowers have the capacity to repay, particularly at a retail level. Selling an ISA requires an assessment, on behalf of the investor, as to the suitability of the product. Selling credit should necessitate the same assessment, not to protect the interests of the bank but to protect the interests of the borrower. We should stop regarding a percentage write off on credit card loans as a cost to banks of extending credit, and we should focus instead on the distress that this bureaucratic indifference causes for individuals and families.

[19] *Creating New Money* Joseph Huber and James Robertson 2000.

Other parts of our financial architecture could also be remodelled. Mortgage finance, for example, could be reset as lease to buy. Or we could include in mortgage contracts a provision that automatically reduces repayments of interest and principal if unemployment levels in a region increase, or house prices fall, by more than an agreed percentage. In so doing, we would reconnect lenders with the wellbeing of the economy and transfer an element of risk back to where it could more readily be absorbed. We could also increase the incentives for long-term fixed rate mortgages.

Reversing debt's tax subsidy

Another signpost towards a lower debt economy would be the abolition of the favourable tax treatment currently given to debt, which in practice results in a tax subsidy being given to one set of taxpayers (mostly business borrowers) by another set of tax payers (everyone else). There are two specific ways in which this happens.

First, trading in debt does not result in a stamp duty (or equivalent) charge. Trading in equity does. This should be reversed.

Secondly, and more materially, at present interest payments are deducted from profits when it comes to calculating the amount of profits that are taxable. No such deduction is made in the case of dividends on equity. This means that, in financial terms, it is preferable to finance a business with debt as opposed to equity. This tax treatment is almost universal around the world, although it is not clear what the justification for it was originally.

Financing a business with debt lent by one group company to another is a technique often used by groups to move taxable profits from a high tax rate jurisdiction to a lower tax rate jurisdiction in order to achieve a decrease in overall rates of taxation. Royalties paid on intellectual property rights (for example, the know-how for manufacturing a particular product) also count as deductions from taxable profits. Together, these two techniques for avoiding tax can significantly deprive a community in which a business is based, and that was the real generating source of profits, of the benefits of the taxation that would otherwise have been paid on them.

More locally, however, the favourable tax treatment given to debt disincentivises equity investment, which is more stable and risk sharing. The UK banks have persuaded us that we must not endanger growth by restricting the ability of banks to lend. This argument would hold considerably less water if equity investment was able to compete on a level playing field. This would be less inflationary and would lead to a greater willingness to invest in productivity and innovation.

Here is Martin Wolf again:

> "...banks should join with other businesses in a campaign to end the distortions in corporate taxation in favour of debt. There is too much debt in the economy. The consequences have been dire."[20]

[20] Martin Wolf *Financial Times* 11 November 2011.

Equity investments could be further encouraged through a more favourable capital gains tax regime for equity securities compared to debt securities, including by gradually reducing the level of tax payable on gains the longer equity securities are held.

Control of politicians

We could also consider some semi-constitutional restraints on government finances to prevent the build up of structural deficits, where there is a fundamental and on-going imbalance between government receipts and expenditure, and a return to fiscal sustainability – but this time based on deliberately cautious, as well as independent, forecasts as to the future.

Politicians who sell us what we want to hear are dangerous, particularly when those whispering loudest in their ears are financiers and large businesses. Much as they might squirm at the prospect, politicians need to be humble enough to accept controls, just as they have had to do in relation to their own expenses, not least so that surpluses are saved rather than spent during the good times to smooth us over more difficult economic cycles. A pre-condition would be a proper distinction between investment and revenue expenditure; borrowing to fund the former being acceptable but borrowing to fund the latter being counter-cyclical with surpluses generated during the up-swings.

Currency alternatives

And we could engage in some serious research about moving towards an asset backed money regime, or even competing forms of currency. It may or may not be desirable to return to the gold standard (although this has been raised as a possibility in the 2012 US Presidential campaign), but a currency backed, for example, by a basket of commodities might be a modern day alternative. An asset backed money system would increase confidence in currencies and government finances, as bondholders would know that governments could no longer print their way out of reckless budget deficits. We may find, in any event, that such a solution is forced upon us, and if so it would be preferable to have considered the pathways in advance. The fiat money system, as we continue to see daily, leads to the temptation to manufacture confetti. In its latest guise, it has tied together in new and untested ways the futures of central banks, private banks, governments and the countries they represent. If our dented trust in fiat money leads to a full scale loss of trust in government credit we may be forced to move at a more uncomfortable pace towards a currency system that is backed by assets that are trusted more than mere promises to pay.

In the meantime, we may see increasing moves by business towards barter (such as oil for resources swaps) as an alternative to discredited currencies. We may also see pressure to allow competing but complimentary currencies that utilise spare capacity and generate local economic growth, without increasing levels of debt, and increase the resilience of the money system to shocks to the national and international financial system. The Swiss already have such a system, known as WIR, operating alongside the Swiss franc and with one fifth of Swiss SMEs participating.

Kicking the habit

As for the connection between leverage and growth it is, of course, ridiculous to imply, as some have done, that there is a straight line connection between the two. For instance, with equity and debt taxed on an equal footing, debt/equity refinancings would become more attractive. Furthermore, growth can also be achieved in other ways. Cutting red tape, making it more attractive to hire staff, encouraging UK businesses to invest their record levels of cash, locally based investments by pension funds and insurance companies, more innovative ways of applying quantitative easing, and higher equity investments by banks following their restructuring into full reserve banks would all off-set the effects of deleveraging. And who wants growth anyway where, as we have seen, most of the benefits of growth are captured by so small a percentage of the population?

The key to kicking the habit of excessive debt is to believe that it is worthwhile and that it is possible. That creates the space needed to imagine things differently, and it provides the energy to find solutions to the objections of those who say it cannot be done. Surely if anything proves that taking money/debt out of the system, and of creating a system in which money/debt cannot accumulate as it has before, it is the events of the last few years. Those preserving the status quo are the ones who need to prove that they are not living in the asylum.

4. Taming speculative and claims-based trading

Excessive trading

Activity in the equity and debt capital markets is increasingly focused on speculative and claims-based trading at the expense of normal investment in fixed interest and equity securities. Now operating on an excessive basis, this is damaging for a number of reasons. The perception among many is that the financial markets have become ever more closely locked into this type of trading for the benefit of market participants at the expense of savers and borrowers.

Claims-based trades: definition

It is worthwhile at this point to define some terms.

Fixed interest securities (corporate bonds, collateralised debt obligations, treasuries, Gilts and so on) are, of course, debt investments. They give rise, therefore, to many of the same concerns as are mentioned in the previous Chapter.

I use the term 'claims-based trades' to refer instead to financial transactions such as equity or debt derivates, credit default swaps (CDSs), currency, commodity and interest rate swaps and futures, and many other hedging strategies. Some claims-based trades are between financial traders and members of the real economy but most are between financial traders. What they share in common with each other, and particularly when they are between financial traders, is no sense of ownership of, responsibility for, or contribution to any underlying business, except for the fixed payments due under the relevant contract establishing the trade.

In this respect claims-based trades are similar to fixed interest securities and other forms of debt. And this is the key reason for concern. Like debt, because they do not depend on the future performance or welfare of their counter-party, nor of the business environment in which that counter-party operates, they create no real incentive to be interested in the welfare of others. Even the notion that one trader might be interested in the welfare of another trader is so strange as to make the point. Sometimes they create an incentive to foster the misfortune of others in the economy.

This divorce in economic concern, particularly when the claims-based trades are between financial traders, has grown, I believe, into both a social and an economic mistake because of the volume of such trades. It does not just isolate traders from the real economy that the finance industry is meant to serve and upon which it is in the end dependent. It creates financial activity that is focused on extracting maximum reward without any accompanying motivation of contribution. It encourages business models, and cultural values, within the sector that seek to extract rather than serve the interests of clients. And it seeks to justify trades by reference merely to the profit of market participants without reference to their adverse societal or market consequences. We will return to these issues in more detail shortly.

Claims-based trades: size of the market

It is difficult to estimate the size of the market in claims-based trading. Hedge Fund Research Inc. estimates that the sums under management by hedge funds grew fourfold between the end of 2000 and the beginning of 2011 and now stand at US$2,000 billion. Some estimates put the volume of currency trading at US$4 trillion, every day. In June 2011 Credit Lime reported a total CDS market volume of US$30 trillion. Popular estimates put the nominal value of claims-based trades at US$600 trillion. That is 40 times the size of the US national debt, itself no small figure. These estimates are not prepared on a consistent basis and may overlap. All that we know is that the elephant is big. US$600 trillion is a lot of firepower to be targeted at something that is not necessarily in the best interests of the economy.

Claims-based trades: betting

Originally the term 'hedge' was reserved for the situation where, for example, a UK business incurred a liability or risk in the normal course of its operations in the real economy, such as a commitment to pay dollars or a need to sell grain, and then hedged the resultant sterling/dollar currency exposure, or the future commodity price risk, through a contract with a third party. Over time, however, the term 'hedge' has come to mean all claims-based trades, whether linked to underlying transactions in the real economy or not. And as the Lex Column in the *Financial Times* put it on 5 June 2012:

> *"…all hedges are essentially bets."*

The difficulty comes in trying to differentiate between different types of bets; those that are helpful to the real economy and those that are either neutral or possibly detrimental. The fact that a bet may also involve an element of skill (remember spot the ball competitions?), as many claims-based trades do, does not stop it from being a bet. Traditionally, society has thought it appropriate to discourage betting for numerous reasons. Indeed, until recently, betting contracts were, as a matter of public policy, legally unenforceable under English law, and a special exemption was needed in financial services legislation to exclude claims-based trades from this general provision.

There is a distinction in terms of social usefulness between the claims-based trade that is hedging a liability or risk of a customer in the real economy, taken on in the normal course of its business, and other forms of claims-based trade. The line between one and the other is notoriously difficult to draw, but the distinction is important.

The distinction should not, however, be used to legitimise imprudent business on the basis that it is 'normal course' business. For example, a bank that grants an imprudent loan because it knows that it can hedge its credit exposure on the borrower through a CDS should not be heard to say that it was merely hedging a risk taken on in the ordinary course of its business. Nor should the distinction be used to legitimise the use by corporates of their treasury funds to engage in betting as an intended profit centre.

It is depressing, if instructive, that the retail spread betting facilities advertised on the London Underground (and accessible via iPhone app), and that thrive on volatility not stability, are allowed a place in modern capital markets. Retail spread betting probably has little effect on economic outcomes. But it is representative of a broader attitude that is at best disinterested in the more serious process of allocating capital.

Much is claimed by the swaps industry in terms of the need to allow the industry to 'innovate'. It is not clear, however, who benefits from this innovation. According to Paul Volcker, the former chair of the US Federal Reserve Bank, the finance industry has in fact invented nothing useful for the real economy for the past 20 years except ATM machines. This may be putting the point too strongly, but those who argue for more 'innovation' do not appear to have come to terms with the fact that the market, left to its own devices, does not necessarily reach beneficial outcomes.

Speculation

Speculation is different to claims-based trading in that it usually involves the purchase or sale of fixed income or equity securities, usually issued by a government or corporate in the real economy. It can, however, carry with it, when occurring on its current scale, the same divorce in economic concern as claims-based trading. As with claims-based trading, this can be both a social and an economic.

In his 1934 seminal work *Security Analysis*, Benjamin Graham was clear about the difference between investment and speculation.[21] Graham defined an investment as something that,

> "upon thorough analysis, promises safety of principal and an adequate return."

Graham also specified a further feature that was important in differentiating between investment and speculation; a sense of ownership of an underlying business. We might now interpret Graham's 'sense of ownership' as connoting a degree of responsibility in terms of stewardship. Anything that was not an investment was, for Benjamin Graham, speculation.

[21] Benjamin Graham went on to write *The Intelligent Investor*, described by Warren Buffet, the world's most successful investor, as the best book on investment ever written.

So the purchase or sale of a security was speculative if it displayed any of the following characteristics:

- if it was made without thorough analysis of the fundamentals of the underlying business

- if it unduly risked capital

- if it sought too high a return, or

- if it showed no sense of ownership of (or responsibility for) an underlying business.

Graham's definition of investment brings within its ambit a good deal of the activity that occurs in modern financial markets, including both short-term and long-term investment. For example, many investment funds are run by managers looking to invest rather than speculate; they may look to buy stocks that are under priced by the market and then to sell them when their prices have begun to exceed underlying value fundamentals. In the meantime, they exercise stewardship over their investments. The difference between investment and speculation is not necessarily one of timescale, although the shorter the time scale the lesser the sense of ownership and therefore the more likely it is that it is speculative.

However, Graham's definition of speculation encompasses a great deal of other activity that occurs in modern financial markets. For example, one important way in which capital can be unduly risked, or that too high a return can be sought, is through the addition of leverage, which can multiply losses as easily as it can multiply profits. Leveraged 'investment' now takes place on a scale that would have been unimaginable to Benjamin Graham. This includes not only investing on the back of borrowed money but also short selling and trading on margins, which amounts to the same thing. [22] Graham would have called leveraged 'investment' on this kind of scale speculation.

High frequency trading, programme trades and exchange traded funds all bear hallmarks of speculation either because of their lack of focus on underlying value fundamentals or because they show no sense of ownership of (or responsibility for) an underlying business. Passive, or index tracking, investments can also look like speculation in some respects. Whilst in theory an index tracking investor should have a sense of ownership, in theory he will seldom engage with the companies in which he is invested because of the costs associated with doing so; a principal reason for index investing being to minimise costs. And in attempting to be average he loses interest in the particular.

The difference between investment and speculation is often dependent upon motivation. One man's investment may be another woman's speculation.

---

[22] Under short selling a trader borrows stock to sell it, betting that he can buy it back at a lower price and profit from the difference. Under naked short selling the trader has not made arrangements to borrow the stock; as a consequence considerably more stock can be sold short and that in turn may materially increase downward pressure on the stock price. Under margin trading, a trader purchasing stock deposits some collateral in respect of part of the purchase price with the broker executing the trade on his behalf but effectively borrows the rest of the price from the broker.

Benefits of speculative and claims based-trades

We should welcome at least some level of speculative and claims-based trading for two reasons. First, because they can meet legitimate demands of the real economy and, second, because they can add to liquidity in the market and help with the price discovery process. We are short of honest scholarship in defining that level, but it is clear that we are considerably beyond it. After that level, we should assess speculative and claims-based trading by reference to their effects not just on traders but also on all of the other actors in the economy and whether parties to the relevant transactions or not.

Potential dangers

Take for example a macro hedge in relation to the economic performance of India. [23] This might enable a trader to benefit from the hard work of Indians as Indian GDP increases. It does little if anything, however, to increase investment in India. It collects a return where there has been no capital risked that might otherwise have produced a social or economic benefit in India. To some this may seem little more than parasitical. On the other side of the trade will be a counter-party who is effectively betting that Indian GDP will decrease. His position may become so large that he is no longer just mildly interested in that result. He may instead be interested in actively pursuing the decline of economic wellbeing in India. That is not in the interests of society (or the conscience of the counter-party). This may seem farfetched in the case of an economy the size of India's. Perhaps less farfetched in the case of a smaller economy.

Trend-following trading in commodities, and the new demand for commodity investment satisfied by commodity indices, have similarly attracted criticism for being contrary to the interests of society, given that they appear both to boost commodity prices and make them more volatile. Likewise short selling (and in particular naked short selling) and CDSs can incentivise traders to seek the destruction of value in others.

Society long ago decided that it was not sensible to allow someone without an interest in a property to insure it because of the temptations to which that could give rise. The same logic has not been applied by regulators to CDSs, many of which are entered into by traders who do not own the underlying debt (or 'property'). A CDS pays out on the occurrence of a 'default event' in relation to a debt, which need not be owned, rather than on the suffering of an actual loss on a debt that is owned. Indeed, under English law, the legal characterisation of a CDS is predicated upon that distinction, because if the trader's intention in entering into the CDS is to receive recompense should he suffer a loss on an asset he owns then the arrangement may be an insurance contract, and that could only be entered into with an insurance company subject to prudential insurance capital requirements. [24] The point is that, by definition, a CDS is legally predicated on no sense of ownership or responsibility.

---

[23] A macro hedge might, for example, be achieved through a combination of claims-based trades linked to currencies, interest rates and government securities.
[24] This form over substance legal rational is not strong at the best of times and is forgotten by traders who do own a debt and are indeed trying to protect themselves against a possible loss by entering into a CDS.

It is also the case that the results of many take-over bids for UK public companies are now heavily influenced, if not determined, by the trading positions taken by arbitrage hedge funds. They generally have little interest in the long-term performance of companies, or of the economies of which they form part. Kraft's takeover of Cadbury, achieved in no small measure because of the stance taken by arbitrage hedge funds, is only one well known example. If one of the purposes of capital markets is to incentivise and encourage good management teams to run businesses for the long-term, then the review that UK Panel on Takeovers and Mergers carried out in relation to the influence of hedge funds on takeovers seems rather half-hearted. It did little to address the problem of short-termist hedge funds with no sense of responsibility towards underlying companies.

The beneficiaries of speculative and claims-based trading

Speculative and claims-based trading is by no means limited to hedge funds. A wide range of financial institutions (including banks and shadow banks and many other market participants) engage in it, and it mostly produces short-term results. Up to half of any profits may go to the individuals who are running the institution and conducting the trades. The losses tend to be borne by the shareholders in the institution, unless of course the losses are so large that the institution becomes insolvent in which case the losses are borne by the institutions that are its creditors. This seems a poor deal from the perspective of the individual savers who are the ultimate end-owners of all financial institutions.

It is also questionable whether much of the 'profit' supposedly created by all this activity is in fact real. The combination of significant volumes of speculative trading, often financed by the debt created by fractional reserve banking, with significant quantities of claims-based trades, creates a huge cloud of financial, non-real assets. Market trading allocates the resultant profits and losses, which net out broadly to zero, between the individual savers who are the ultimate end-owners of all investments. In the process, little has been achieved in the real economy, or for savers when looked at as a whole, except for the capture by the financial services sector of fees for having expanded, shuffled and re-dealt the deck of cards.

The net results for commercial clients in the real economy dealing with claims-based traders are also not what they might be. Research has shown that even competitive agents, such as financial traders, are able to extract progressively higher rents from increasingly complex financial arrangements (as claims-based trades frequently are) to the point where the agents are capturing the bulk of any gain, usually because of information asymmetry.[25]

Adverse effects on the market

It has long been recognised that excessive speculative and claims-based trading may cause market price difficulties. For example, it increases the tendency of asset prices to boom in a period of credit expansion, and it increases their tendency to collapse in a period of de-leveraging. It increases the level of price correlation between assets in the same sector, and it increases the level of price correlation between assets in different sectors. It creates dark pools of capital trading at prices that are not visible to the market, and it creates the temptation to engage in financial transactions simply to earn fees for activity. All of these damage the capital allocation process and obscure the ability of the market to follow high-performing executive management teams.

Speculative trading depends in the main on returns from gains in asset prices. It has little interest in the quality or quantity of revenue income – even though, in the end, it is only that income that determines value. This further erodes the connection between price and fundamental value and encourages financial engineering by corporates that adds little to long-term value.

SPECULATION

Speculative and claims-based trading also creates integrity risks to the structure of the markets. The Financial Services Authority (the FSA) concluded in July 2011 that the risk to financial stability through the hedge fund market (and this is not the entirety of the speculative and claims-based trading market) was limited. However, this does not address the fact that sub-prime debt crisis would not have arisen were it not for the claims-based trading market that packaged, divided and 'guaranteed' collateralised debt obligations and their attendant risks.

[25] Biais, Rochet and Wooley 2009.

The FSA report in July 2011 also commented that systemic risks remained if hedge funds were unable to manage a sudden withdrawal of liabilities during a stressed market environment, potentially resulting in forced asset sales. If this were to occur across a number of funds, or in one large highly leveraged fund, then it could cause pressure on market liquidity and efficient pricing.

High frequency trading has just about managed to escape the blame for the flash crash in May 2010 that reduced share prices by US$650 billion in 30 minutes. Still no one really knows why that happened. One theory, however, is that it was caused by unpredictable, unknowable and uncontrollable technological systems interacting with other similarly complex technological systems through the medium of speculative and claims-based trading.

One of the difficulties in addressing speculative and claims-based trading is that each individual trade, on its own, may seem relatively harmless to others whilst being beneficial to the trader. Why should I be discouraged from doing something I want when it appears to be harmless to others? But this ignores the systemic effect. It may be acceptable for one person, and perhaps even two, to pick a wild flower but if everyone does it then soon the hedgerows are bare. One trade on its own may well be harmless, but when combined with thousands of others it may contribute to, or cause, a financial disaster. One issue of collateralised debt obligations containing a limited amount of sub-prime mortgages may have been manageable. On mass they were not manageable. And it was not just that sub-prime debt was itself a poor investment. The systemic effect of the collapse in the sub-prime market was to wreak havoc on numerous neighbouring markets because of the interconnectivity of modern day finance.

There is greater transparency growing in the market, but progress is slow. It is still the case that some investors in hedge funds have little or no idea as to how they operate, and indeed hedge funds have traditionally made the opacity of their black boxes a selling point in a masterful stroke of reverse psychology when marketing to investors (as per Bernie Madoff). Transparency is improving, but it remains the case that opacity runs counter to all good principles of stewardship, not least because it makes impossible any connection between an investor and his investment in the same way that de-coupling voting rights from economic interests does when it comes to certain forms of stock lending. Many opaque swap based exchange traded funds (ETFs) promoted by investment banks provide an inexpensive way for investment banks to borrow cash in return for less liquid collateral. They are far from being the simple products that at first they may appear. It seems only a matter of time before there are claims of misselling of synthetic ETFs to rival those of the split capital trusts.

Leaning into the wind

Classification of speculative and claims-based trading as either 'good' or 'bad' is unhelpful. Not only are there no clear lines, but even when lines can be drawn between trades the same trade may have different effects when employed in a different context with a different motivation and with a different aggregate value. And, as noted, there is a level of speculative and claims-based trading that does add, in a beneficial way, to the real economy and the proper functioning of the market.

The answer to excessive speculative and claims-based trading is not, therefore, to prevent it. It is to lean against it. Some or all of the following are ways in which that might be done:

- draw a distinction between:
  - claims-based trades that are in substance insurance against the possibility of a loss on an asset (or an increase in a commitment) that is owned (or incurred) by the buyer of the protection as part of its normal business in the real economy ('real economy trades'), and
  - claims-based trades that are not real economy trades ('financial trades'),
- introduce increased capital requirements for banks selling real economy trades or financial trades,
- apply insurance type capital requirements to non-banks selling real economy trades or financial trades,
- introduce a ban on financial trades unless the regulators are persuaded that:
  - the trades will not result in unacceptable risks to the market if adopted on a broad basis, and
  - the trades will provide material benefits to end savers, borrowers and the real economy rather than simply market participants,
- introduce or apply increased transaction taxes to speculative and claims-based trading,
- apply increased corporate tax rates on profits made from speculative and claims-based trading,
- introduce a ban on naked short selling,
- adjust market trading rules so as to implement all purchases (and sales) of securities made within a given time frame at the same price, thus removing the incentive for high frequency trading which seeks an advantage by having its trades implemented first before others can trade,
- lean against debt (commonly used to finance speculative trading) as described in the previous Chapter, and
- lean in favour of long-term equity investment as described in the next Chapter.

Investors might also take more responsibility by discouraging financial institutions from entering into speculative and claims-based trades unless and until the remuneration structures of those institutions align better with the long-term horizons of most investors, in particular by deferring the rewards of individual traders until the more long-term consequences of their trades have had an opportunity to unfold.

However, because of the difficulties of definition, and because of the importance of motivation in determining the distinctions, an equally powerful, if not more powerful, tool in taming speculative and claims-based trades is strong leadership by the management of financial institutions. There is no need for leaders to wait until regulatory changes are introduced before applying the principles outlined above to their businesses.

The effect on cultures and behaviours

Speculative and claims-based trading, like debt, creates a particular stance in relation to the future. Over-strenuous attempts to insulate oneself against both the uncertainties of the future, and to remove any need to rely on anyone other than oneself, is, as we have observed earlier, a mistake. If I think that I am in control of my future, and can flourish without the need for any relationships with others, I am in danger of being either arrogant or foolish, or both. The impression provided in recent years by sophisticated computer models giving false comfort as to future cash flows only adds to the self-delusion.

What may once have been a conscious decision to leave to clients the responsibility for deciding upon the social consequences of the funding provided by the City has in recent years turned instead into something else: a blindness as to the existence of any wider social, environmental or economic consequences of the City's activities, including its consequences for the City's own staff.

Many have wondered why bankers and traders, who include amongst their number many of the brightest minds in the world, missed the signs that might have warned them about the impending banking crisis of 2007-08. Many have wondered why banks, and the hedge funds that are their cultural satellites, have a tendency to create ruthless internal cultures. And, although it would be unfair to lay all of the blame at their feet, it is concerning that the influence of these firms creates a cultural paradigm that others tend to follow both in the City and beyond.

I believe that, first, the over-confidence and, second, the relational isolationism that are the product of a debt based industry, fuelled by speculative and claims-based trades, are two of the most significant factors that led to this failure to foresee the coming crisis. Debt and speculative and claims-based trades tend to be zero sum games, where your gain is my loss. So it also becomes important that I permit you as little gain as possible. And the instability of the current bank funding model, where every bank is a day away from insolvency should depositors decide to remove their cash, leads to an environment where control is the only rational response. Taken together, these factors produce management cultures that are aggressive and utilitarian. Too big to manage, not just financially but also humanely.

Bankers and traders may not seem an obvious target for sympathy at the moment, but there is growing evidence that a mental health crisis is developing in the financial services industry. One health insurer, Legal & General, reported in January 2012 that mental health claims were responsible for 44 per cent of all health claims by workers in financial services and insurance, considerably higher than the average.

This is not surprising given the characteristics needed to compete, for example, in a typical investment banking team. One survey described these characteristics as a first class education, a craving for money, a great deal of testosterone, and a deep-seated passion for winning and obtaining control. [26]

One of the tragedies of the financial crisis has been the demonsing in the public imagination of a workforce that was in many quarters already under enormous stress. Excessive bonuses have been widely criticised. What has been less commented on, however, is a culture that uses discretionary bonuses, which by definition are not a contractual entitlement, as a tool to avoid meeting the normal obligations of an employer when dismissing staff. What has also been less recognised is a culture that threatens, on a daily basis, to withhold a bonus in order to obtain relentless and outstanding performance and with no respect for the family or social life of potential recipients. Action is needed to reform the finance industry if for no reason other than to protect its employees.

The irony is that the isolation that this culture produces dulls the commercial judgment of the banker or trader. Increasingly cut off from the normal world, he can no longer appreciate the impact of broader societal trends on the decisions he is making because he can no longer see those trends. Nor, increasingly, can he appreciate the consequences of his decisions on the society in which he lives.

In *A Week in December* Sebastian Faulks' character Vanessa Veals reflects on the work of her husband John, a successful trader, and their life together in London:

> *"...banking became a closed system. Profit was no longer related to growth or increase, but became self-sustaining; and in this semi-virtual world, the amount of money to be made by financiers also became unhitched from normal logic.*

[26] Joris Luyendijk's *Banking Blog* on the Guardian website after a nine month anthropological survey.

It followed, Vanessa thought, that the people who could flourish here must themselves be, in some profound and personal way, detached. They could have no qualms about the effects of what they did; no cares for the collateral impact – although, to do them justice, they did take precautions to minimise the possibility of any contact with reality; indeed the joy of the new products was exactly their magical self-sufficiency, the way they appeared to eliminate the risk of any final reckoning. However, it remained necessary for these people to have – or to develop very quickly – a very limited sense of 'the other'; a kind of functional autism was the ideal state of mind.

Some people thought the crux of it was the invention of some credit derivative products by a few people at J.P. Morgan; but in fact, in Vanessa's mind, the key was that society as a whole in London and New York had so lost its bearings that it was prepared to believe, with these analysts, that cause and effect could be uncoupled. To her, this social change, the result of decades of assault on long-accepted norms, was far more interesting than the quasi-autistic intellects of the people, like John, who worked in the new finance."

This portrait is a caricature, but like many a caricature it carries an element of truth. We owe it to society, and to those who work in the City, to stop the caricature from prevailing.

Repentance and forgiveness

Banks are far from being the only actors at fault in the lead up to the credit crisis of 2007-08 and from which we continue to suffer. There was a failure of foresight and prudence on a considerable scale by nearly the whole political, academic, financial, business and media community. Consumers must also share the blame for having consumed too much and borrowed too much. A flawed currency union has compounded the difficulties in Europe.

Most bankers in the lead up to the crisis were working honestly and hard to do the best job they could. Nevertheless, banks are to be applauded for having apologised for the role they played, although other market participants have been slower to acknowledge their role in the collective short-sightedness that led to the crisis. There does, however, seem to be some confusion amongst banks and other market participants as to the meaning of 'repentance' and 'forgiveness', and as to the connections between the two.

Repentance involves more than an apology, even a heart-felt and genuine one. Repentance involves not just sorrow but a change of mind; a decision to walk in an opposite direction and not go down the previous path. Repentance also involves restitution, an attempt to put right any damage caused. Repentance does not lead to a right to forgiveness. That is the free choice of those who have been hurt. It is not clear that the finance industry has fully taken this on board yet.

Forgiveness is an extraordinarily powerful tool, and it does not need to wait to be given until the one who has caused the hurt offers an apology. Forgiveness can be impactful on the one being forgiven, but it can be even more releasing for the one who is providing the forgiveness. There are, however, a number of things that forgiveness need not entail. Forgiveness does not mean that what happened did not matter, nor that broken trust must immediately be restored. Nor does it mean that the one providing the forgiveness must allow the one who has caused the hurt to keep hold of the tools by which the hurt was caused. That would be naïve. It is not clear that the finance industry has fully understood this either.

The necessary degree of change in the finance industry is unlikely to come from the current leadership of City and Wall Street banks. They grew in the same stable as the leaders who took us into the financial crisis. They genuinely and in good faith believe that, subject to some minor adjustments and some training in ethics, the way things were is the best way for them to be. I believe them to be wrong.

5. Bi-productive investment

The purpose of markets

The interim Kay Review of UK Equity Markets and Long-Term Decision Making describes the objective of the financial markets as being the efficient allocation of capital, worked out in practice in two ways. First, by securing the public purposes of high performing companies, and strong returns to savers, through an effective asset management industry. And, secondly, by ensuring that corporate profits are translated into returns to beneficiaries by minimising the costs of intermediation. Liquidity, transparency and price discovery should not be ends in themselves, but should be intermediate objectives that support the principal purpose of markets.

Despite the many benefits delivered by today's financial markets, they are now displaying a number of signs that call into question the extent to which they are fulfilling this objective. If they are not then neither the interests of the private individuals who are the real owners of all capital, nor the interests of the businesses in which they are invested, are being as well served as they might be.

The list of difficulties is long. It includes short-termism that discourages long-term planning and investment; financial engineering to improve performance against financial measures but with no particular benefit for the real economy; multi-layered structures between investors, advisors, managers and companies that multiply principal/agent conflicts relating to business objectives, financial performance and fees; remuneration structures within institutions that misalign interests; fees and trading practices that are reflective of oligopolistic markets; and increasing levels of price correlation between and across sectors that are destructive of fundamental valuation and attempts to diversify risk.

As the interim Kay Report says, there is a mismatch between the business models of asset managers and the interests of companies and beneficiaries. Or as the *Financial Times* has commented:

> *"Concern is… growing that the markets are morphing into little more than a playground for a specialised type of trading that has minimal economic benefit and contributes little if anything to capital formation – the traditional function of stock exchanges."* [27]

In short, the City is in danger of no longer being trusted by either savers or borrowers as a fair or efficient market in which to operate.

[27] *Financial Times* 2 September 2010.

I believe, however, that the investment community (of which we are all part if we are savers or pensioners) is suffering from two other and more foundational problems. They both result from the investment markets having forgotten the paradox of profit. We have sought to extract too much, and to contribute too little.

The paradox of profit

The mantra of the investment markets is maximising returns commensurate with risk (although there is some irony in the shareholder spring having targeted directors who have applied that mantra to their own remuneration). The real economy, however, knows that profit does not come from seeking to maximise one's own reward. Rather it is through the process of contributing to the needs and preferences of customers that profit is achieved on a long-term and growing basis. This is the paradox of profit. Business understands that it must give in order to receive, and that if its primary focus is on maximising returns it will alienate its customers and damage its earnings.

Maximising returns commensurate with risk has led to a series of unfortunate motivations and practices. It has led to a utilitarian view of the markets, with investors seeing them as being there merely to serve their own interests. And it has led to a focus on financial statistics divorced from the business of business. Examples abound: the confusion of value between immediate mark-to-market trading price and long-term investment value; risk being seen merely in terms of price volatility rather than the adventure of business decisions; disinterest in stewardship amongst investors and market participants; a sense of entitlement to reward rather than thankfulness for the custom of stakeholders; and financial activity that contributes little if anything to the real economy.

Bi-productive investment

If we are over focused on extraction we are also under focused on contribution. A friend of mine recently gave his daughter a large sum of money. She went to see an investment manager, who spotted that she was politically aware. Most of the conversation that ensued was, therefore, about the things in which she should not invest. When the young woman got home she said to her father:

> "Dad, all he talked about was what <u>not</u> to do with my money. But what I want to do is to do something <u>useful</u> with my money."

YOUR ASSETS ARE CURRENTLY ON MARS

Sometimes it takes someone unused to conventional wisdom to see its shortcomings. The issue she was raising is both simple and fundamental. Too many of us are, as investors, merrily orbiting the earth in our financial satellites – adjusting our mathematical vectors and rocket boosters – unconnected and uninterested in what is going on down below us on planet earth.

Too many of us see the markets as little more than the place where we put our money on the table. What happens underneath the table, so to speak, most of us neither know nor care. The 'efficient allocation of capital', like so many other economic maxims, can short-change both our imaginations and our rationality.

In the words of John Authers, the *Financial Times'* senior investment columnist:

> *"The ideal, which takes different forms, would be to move away from a quantitative and mathematical approach and return to investing. Rather than 'rationality', or a belief in markets that are 'efficient', some economists now call for a return to 'reason'. Investors and managers must start using their own judgement."* [28]

I believe that one of the keys to returning to rational investing is to see the markets in a different light and look for investment that is productive twice; once at the other end of the investment chain in terms of producing a social benefit through the goods, services and operations of investee companies, and once at the investor end of the investment chain in terms of producing a reasonable finance return. This is what I call 'bi-productive investment'.

And by reasonable return, I mean a return that does not always seek to squeeze the last pip out of the lemon. A relentless drive by business solely to maximise its revenue breaks the paradox of profit and becomes self-defeating. Likewise, a relentless drive by investors to maximise their returns, when that message is transmitted by the capital markets to business, eventually destroys the very thing it wishes to see prosper.

GOOD FOR ME – GOOD FOR YOU

[28] John Authers *Boldness in Business* 21 March 2012.

There is a saying in Gaelic:

"Fas a' ghruinnd a reir an uachdarain."
(The yield of the ground is according to the landlord, and by implication not the tenant.)

If we (the landlords) as savers and pensioners instruct our investment managers and pension funds to maximise our returns we should not be surprised when our communities and families, and perhaps including ourselves as customers and employees, feel the costs of that strategy as companies (our tenants) put that policy into effect.

We do not want farms that produce at the edge of the envelope; no matter what the season or the weather producing food to their maximum capacity and without regard to what that means in terms of soil fatigue, animal welfare, bio diversity, disease resilience, and frankly sheer enjoyment of the countryside. In the end, a farm run at the edge of the envelope will die of exhaustion. We do not want that in farming. We should not want it in investing.

Purposeful business

Some would say that business needs a more rounded understanding of how it can and does create permanent value. In 1975 only 17 per cent of the market capitalisation of the S&P 500 was made up by forms of capital other than physical and financial capital; that 17 per cent being what we would now call human, natural and social capital. By 2009, the proportion of the market capitalisation of the S&P 500 made up by the value of human, natural and social capital had risen to over 80 per cent. [29]

The understanding of the investment markets as to the complex and interconnected processes by which this value is created is, however, still surprisingly immature, even despite this rise large in valuation and even though many in business understand the process more fully. The investment markets still struggle to recognise anything other than today's share price and this frustrates a deeper understanding for four reasons. First, in theory today's share price is the discounted value of future income streams, but in practice today's share price is influenced by a whole host of factors unconnected to that income. Second, the very fact of discounting discounts the factors upon which that income is dependent. Third, the calculation says little about the nature or depth of the relationships making up the human, natural and social capital that produces the income, even before discounting their value. And fourth, the value of human, natural and social capital is still not represented in the financial statements of companies, and what is not measured, in the eyes of many, does not count. The philosophy of finance, trumpeted loudly by the capital markets, militates against the compelling logic of long-term decision making in business. Our efforts to reduce everything that is of value to a single price point have not only failed, they have also misled us. It is time to give up on the attempt and learn to value what we value in more sophisticated ways.

[29] *Integrated Reporting* September 2011.

If we want to contribute, as well as receive, when we invest, and so benefit through the paradox of profit on a long-term and consistent basis, then we need to invest in what I call 'purposeful business'.

A purposeful business will first and foremost seek to meet the needs and preferences of customers, and seek to build permanent value represented by financial, physical, human, natural and social capital, recognising the complex and interwoven forces at work in so doing. A purposeful business will do the right thing for the business in terms of promoting these varied forms of capital even if that is neither recognised nor rewarded (at least in the short-term) by the equity and debt capital markets. By seeking first to serve the interests of customers, generosity will always be a feature in the business models of purposeful businesses.

There are calls for business to become more sustainable, and this is commonly understood as business that meets the needs of today without compromising the ability of future generations to meet their own needs. The definition of environmental sustainability for the purposeful business is one of care and respect for the natural world, not one of managing resources as close to the margin as seems technically possible.

Purposeful business avoids the assumption made by some (even if incorrectly) that sustainability is only about environmental matters. It is more aspirational in its objectives for humanity than the sustainability tag might imply. It questions the needs and preferences of today and asks whether the goods and services being offered are of genuine benefit to individuals and communities. Purposeful business looks for human development, fulfilment and wellbeing.

Some may wish to add a further element to the definition of purposeful business; on occasion the business will step beyond market failures. In this context, a market failure includes a situation in which, even though legal, it pays a company in the long run to do the wrong thing in societal or environmental terms. It also includes a situation in which, even though legal, it pays a company in the long run not to do the right thing. So on occasion a purposeful business may choose not to pursue a profitable opportunity, simply because it believes it is the wrong thing to do. Or on occasion a purposeful business may choose to benefit society or the environment entirely gratuitously, simply because it believes it is the right thing to do. A purposeful business will not always seek to maximise its externalities, adopting a more socially conscious yardstick as the measure for its conduct than the law or the utilitarian philosophy of accounting.

BUSINESS AS JAZZ

It follows that purposeful businesses are likely to be led by men and women with a clear sense of mission, supported by strong and positive values, and well able to communicate and operationalise their vision.

To help us, we may need a new metaphor for business and its connection with the society of which it forms part, including other businesses. The invisible hand is past its sell-by date, not least because the picture it paints is too individualistic. Business as jazz may be a more useful metaphor: an orchestra of different players, both within and alongside each business, each weaving their harmonies into the rhythm of the whole; every participant aware of and responding to the contribution of the others; each instrument making its own unique contribution. One song. Many voices.

Bi-productive investment is not an either/or investment strategy, where the investor must choose between financial returns and social effects. It is a both/and strategy where the investor expresses an interest in both of those outcomes and understands their interconnectivity.

In summary, therefore, bi-productive investment seeks to put capital to productive use by investing in purposeful business. And a reasonable financial return for the investor, produced by the paradox of profit, is the reward for so doing. At present, however, those wishing to invest bi-productively have too little information upon which to base their decisions. This is a point to which we will return in a moment. First, however, we will look at some of the consequences that might flow from an investment universe that has moved towards bi-productive investment.

Creating the future

How and where we invest helps to create the future, for good or ill.

For too long we have, I believe, divorced our investment decisions from our concern for the context in which we live, believing that we have no responsibility for the operations that are funded by our pensions and savings. We have certainly not been encouraged to think along those lines by those who advise us on how to invest. If we have ever come close to the issue we have probably only been asked whether we want to be an 'ethical' investor, which for many usually means simply selecting a number of stocks, like genetically modified food producers or animal tested drug companies, into which we do not wish to invest.

But being a bi-productive investor focused on the productive deployment of capital is not about being an ethical investor in these narrow terms. It is about making positive decisions about where best to invest based on a more sophisticated and blended series of criteria. For Aristotle, one of the key aims of virtue was to help one become a fully flourishing member of the political process, and in particular through how one engaged in civic life. However, it is now business, not just politics, that plays a key role in national affairs. Maybe Aristotle would now see one of the key aims of virtue as being to help savers become fully flourishing members of the business process through how they invest.

Some will not accept that there is any connection between virtuous intention and investment, and they will contend that they have an unfettered right to invest without regard to any social or environmental consequences. This is, however, another economic and social mistake of the kind highlighted in Chapter 4. It misunderstands the nature of the profit making process, and it overstates the moral rights associated with private property.

Most of us have grown up in a culture that regards a person's rights to his or her property as being an absolute moral claim that excludes all other moral considerations. Private property need not, however, be seen in such binary terms. Families, for example, have a more nuanced understanding of the nature of private property. Grandpa, for instance, may be wealthy, but there is a reasonable expectation that he will not squander his wealth so that his children have nothing left to inherit. We do not regard the right to roam over moorland, or the right to lay utility cables under back gardens, as attacking the rights of private property. These expectations do not compete with the rights of ownership, nor do they argue for common ownership. They simply provide a more subtle and communal understanding of private property.

It ought not to be a surprising notion, therefore, that when it comes to investing we should have regard to the social and environmental consequences of our investment choices. There are consequences, and we have a responsibility for them. Philanthropy has its place, but it is better to invest in an employer who provides a decent wage than it is to provide charity to the employee's family.

Effects of bi-productive investment

A change towards bi-productive investment would affect the world of investment in numerous ways.

It would, of course, continue to encourage investment in many of the businesses in which we are currently invested, not least because they are selling goods and services that meet genuine needs, but it might discourage investment in others. If we had a choice, for example, between investing in two broadly comparable mining companies, it might encourage investment in the one with the better human rights record. If we had a choice between investing in two roughly similar food manufacturing businesses, it might encourage investment in the one that was doing more to tackle obesity. It might foster investment into sectors currently struggling to find sufficient private sector finance, such as clean energy and less profitable drugs for low income world diseases (although it is encouraging to see some pharmaceutical companies tackling this already). And it would provide us with a broader range of tools with which to differentiate between the earnings of companies in different sectors. It might lead us to shun gambling companies in exchange for other industries with similar cash flows but more beneficial social outcomes, and it might lead us to disinvest from tobacco companies in favour of other less damaging defensive stocks.

Changes in investor preference would, in accordance with the laws of supply and demand, decrease the cost of capital, by increasing the stock price, of the more socially and environmentally beneficial companies. It would also increase the cost of capital, by decreasing the stock price, of those thought to be less beneficial.

The change would cut through the current debates about fiduciary duty within the investment management industry. At present even those trustees and managers who do take environmental, social and governance issues into account only feel permitted to do so to the extent that they believe they positively impact financial performance. Much of the investment management industry adheres to the argument that its overriding duty is to maximise financial returns on behalf of its clients and beneficiaries and nothing else. The change would, however, bypass this discussion because individual investors, the beneficial owners on whose behalf such fiduciary duties are exercised, would be empowered to instruct their managers and trustees that they wanted issues relating to human, social and natural capital taken into account on their own merits, and not merely in so far as they impacted financial outcomes. Of course, institutional investors who were persuaded that financial value could not be separated from human, social and natural capital would do so anyway.

The effects on the investment management industry could also be profound. The decision making process of many asset managers, including pension funds and insurance companies, is heavily influenced by statisticians and actuaries with little expertise in the business of business. Skilled as they may be professionally, they have little experience of making commercial judgements about whether new products might excite or disappoint customers or about the broader range of forms of capital that bi-productive investment encapsulates. They have the prime seat at the table, and they steer the conversation towards sectoral asset allocation and hypothetical returns, not individual investments and specific implications. We should not quickly forget that the economic theories of rational expectations and efficient markets failed to predict or prevent the financial crisis or the massive loss of share values that followed. And it is now clear that there are no risk free assets. Models that pretend otherwise are just as likely to misallocate capital as good old fashioned business judgement.

If bi-productive investment became the dominant philosophy the investment management industry would have to adapt both to reflect more closely the concerns and interests of its clients, who might be interested in social and environmental impacts simply on their own terms, and to reflect the more nuanced understanding that would develop about the constituent elements of long-term value creation. Its heroes might no longer be mathematicians and nuclear physicists who can construct ever more intricate trading strategies. They might become social and environmental experts who can best advise how to channel private sector finance for the benefit of both society and investors. In particular, we might see greater efforts being devoted by the investment management community to social and environmental agendas beyond simply global warming, including as regards bio-diversity and the ecosystems (water, forests, fish and soil) on which humanity depends. We might also see more focus on the growth of businesses that develop the capacity of individuals and communities. And we as investors might appreciate more warmly those fund managers who are able to work closely with businesses that are seeking to develop and implement long-term and sustainable strategies.

Hopefully, the change would also help to dethrone the tyranny of benchmark investing. Given a wider range of desired outcomes, keeping up with the Joneses in terms of a financial strategy would cease to be so relevant. Instead, investment managers would be incentivised to differentiate themselves around a wider range of positive outcomes, rather than herd around a measure that some would say is designed more to protect managers from criticism and the loss of client mandates than it is to produce long-term, real returns for clients. Over correlated markets should mean that there are pricing inefficiencies in relation to the fundamental valuation of companies, but among many managers the focus of attention is at present more on macroeconomic forces and effectively index tracking investment strategies because of their lack of appreciation of the factors that drive genuine business growth.

Significantly, moving towards bi-productive investment would re-connect investors with their investments, and perhaps this would be the most profound change of all. Our current investment arrangements mean that we are disconnected from where our money is invested. Few of us could name the top 10 companies in which our savings and pensions are invested. With that level of knowledge it is no wonder that we do not care what the companies do with our money, how they treat their staff, or how they handle environmental challenges. With bi-productive investment, care and interest stand at the beginning of the investment process and are not left as possible by-products that are in practice usually forgotten.

Connecting investors with the purposes to which their capital is put would radically reform notions of stewardship. We would see an investment environment develop that was far less short-term as investors came to appreciate that time is needed to produce and sustain financial, social and environmental benefits.

In turn, this would transform the objectives and incentives of company directors and business managers, who would no longer find themselves under pressure to manage for short-term financial outcomes rather than invest in research, development and productivity. Businesses would develop a clearer sense of purpose, and a greater understanding of their social usefulness, and this would lead to improved staff moral and engagement. Well run businesses would develop systems and policies for identifying and mitigating negative impacts, and for developing and magnifying positive impacts. They would be clearer at board level about corporate objectives and about communicating those objectives internally and externally. Decisions would not be made simply by 'having regard' to non-financial criteria. Those criteria would also have a seat in the decision making process.

Traditional corporate social responsibility (CSR) strategies, always tempted to focus on philanthropic activities, would continue to play a role in business life. There would, however, be a greater recognition that the greatest good that a company can do already lies within its existing operations – the way in which it conducts its normal business, including its externalities.

International and local investment

Bi-productive investment would also re-connect us with the welfare of our national and more local communities.

Business investment over the last 10 years as a share of gross domestic product is second lowest in the UK among advanced economies, and in recent years the picture has been deteriorating. If we want to see an increase in high-tech manufacturing and an expansion of creative industries in the UK then surely it is down to us as UK investors to help this happen. If we want to see a change in our economy from quantitative growth to qualitative improvement, so that our economy becomes better, for example, at cutting carbon emissions and increasing the quality of its productivity, then surely it is down to us as investors to steer this process. It is estimated that UK companies are currently holding around £750 billion in cash. Many would like to see that invested in the UK economy.

It is tempting to be persuaded by the logic of the free movement of capital across national boundaries, which seems to be in contradiction to the benefits of local investment. Many have, I suspect, been persuaded by the argument that everyone benefits from free trade and we assume that the same applies to the free movement of capital. In fact, there are both economic and social shortcomings in the free trade argument.

The economist David Ricardo is generally assumed to have proved the economic case for free trade between different countries back in 1817. However, his proof was based on the premise that capital was immobile, as of course it was in the early 19th century. Capital now flows freely to the countries with absolute advantage, undermining his assumption that comparative advantage between countries could be maintained because capital would continue to support an industry that gave comparative if not absolute advantage.

Although free trade benefits the business with global reach, it is not so clear that it always benefits the high income country from which its manufacturing is outsourced. Nor is it clear that it always benefits the low income country that is increasingly encouraged to lose diversity of occupation. It encourages the former to live beyond its natural capacity, so increasing environmental degradation, and encourages the latter to act as the sink for the externalities of the former, including fewer welfare benefits and lower health and safety standards.

Free trade may be beneficial when there is fair competition; it is less obviously fair to some businesses in the West when their competitors in the East compete not on the basis of lower costs, just because they have lower welfare standards, but on the basis of lower costs because they have inadequate welfare standards. It is, of course, the right of Eastern nations to determine their own welfare standards. That does not, however, mean that we in the West need to accept the consequences of them doing so, or at least not on the grounds of free (presumably also meant to be fair) trade.

Nor is it clear in any event that free trade has brought us all of the advantages in the West that are often assumed, particularly if one has regard to measures of overall welfare rather than just gross domestic product. It is not clear that overall welfare in the UK, measured in terms of health, education, opportunity, employment and social cohesion, has improved as a result of free trade's contribution to GDP over the last half century.

Those who argue in favour of free trade point to the millions lifted out of poverty in the East by the effects of globalisation. Who knows, however, whether China would by now have a democratic government that did not deny basic human rights and political freedoms, and cause environmental devastation, if the West had not outsourced its manufacturing to the Far East. Who knows whether the West would have been saved a financial crisis and a decade, at least, of stagnant growth if the Chinese savings arising from the resultant trading imbalance had not been invested in our financial system. Who knows what reduced pressures there would be on energy resources and carbon emissions if goods travelled less far from production to market.

Nor should free trade in goods and services be confused with the free flow of money across national borders. The two are not necessarily the same. Samuel Brittan put it as follows when describing how to tame finance:

> *"It is… a matter of recognising, at every point of policy decision, that the free movement of artificially created money across frontiers is not on a par with the free movement of goods and services, let alone more basic human freedoms, and recognising this not only for developing countries but for the so-called advanced ones as well."* [30]

All the more remarkable, perhaps, given that in 1998 Samuel Brittan was describing exchange controls as *"one of the most potent forms of tyranny"* that can be used by a state to imprison its citizens. Emerging markets over the last decade have experienced huge capital inflows. Many policy makers in those countries are now concerned about their inflationary and potentially destabilising effects.

These points are not made to argue the case against the free movement of capital and trade. They are made to emphasise that it should not simply be assumed that by investing into emerging or foreign markets one is necessarily making a more moral choice because of the benefits of allocating capital 'efficiently'. I will leave it to others to argue the case for and against capital controls, much of which depends on your view as to the merits or otherwise of state power versus private finance power. I am simply making the case for voluntary national and local investment. Even leaving aside the risks of investing in a foreign and therefore unfamiliar market, there are plenty of good economic, environmental and social reasons for investing money nationally and locally.

Bi-productive investment might also offer the UK some increased protection against the disinterest of foreign owners in the wellbeing of the UK communities in which mega-businesses operate. Because UK institutional investors are currently focused almost entirely on financial returns, and one might argue have become divorced from the interests of their UK clients in terms of the general welfare of the society in which they live, UK institutional investors have been steadily increasing their asset allocations to overseas markets and decreasing their investments in the equity of UK companies. This might be sensible from a purely short to medium-term financial perspective. It is less obviously beneficial from a long-term social and financial perspective. The bi-productive agenda might reverse that trend.

[30] Samuel Brittan *Financial Times* 10 June 2011.

Integrated reporting and advice

To create an environment in which bi-productive investment can be seriously pursued it is necessary for investors to be provided with the right information. This means that business needs to produce it, and that the investment management industry needs to engage with it. This may not be as unwelcome to business as it might first appear. It should enable business to gain greater recognition for the steps it takes to create long-term value. The investment management industry may find the process more challenging, given its current focus and reward structures.

Probably the most significant development underway at present in this field is the work of the International Integrated Reporting Council (the IIRC). The IIRC is seeking to create a new mainstream corporate reporting model, known as integrated reporting, that identifies, measures and reports on what it defines as financial, manufactured, human, intellectual, natural and social capital. [31] It is committed to doing so in a manner that recognises the interconnectivity of these factors and demonstrates the relationship between a corporate's business model and these various forms of capital. The reports would be prepared according to consistent measures and would be independently verified.

The work of the IIRC is gaining significant support around the world. It will be some time before its work is complete, and it has significant challenges to overcome. But if the project can be brought to successful completion it will represent a very significant step forward in providing a meaningful assessment of the purposeful nature, environmental sustainability and long-term viability (or otherwise) of a business.

Armed with this information, investors would be able to weigh up the relative advantages and disadvantages of particular investments from a social and environmental perspective as well as from a financial perspective.

Regulatory support

Four regulatory changes are needed to support integrated reporting and bi-productive investment.

First, listed companies need to be required to produce integrated reports. An initiative led by Aviva Investors for the 2012 Earth Summit is seeking an international commitment to require listed companies to report annually on sustainability in adherence with four principles: annual disclosure on environmental and social issues on a comply or explain basis, effective measures to enable investors to hold companies to account, boards to set company objectives and values to align with the interests of stakeholders, and remuneration structures to be implemented that reflect these objectives.

[31] For more definition of these terms see *Towards Integrated Reporting Communicating Value in the 21st Century* September 2011.

Eventually, this may lead to integrated reporting in the manner envisaged by the IIRC, but in the meantime companies can voluntarily decide to prepare and publish relevant information. Professor John Ruggie has demonstrated with his UN Guiding Principles for the implementation of his 'Protect, Respect and Remedy' human rights framework that the adoption of new laws is not the only way to make progress in complex areas. Soft law initiatives and stakeholder encouragement can also play a strong role in increasing awareness, changing behaviours, and improving performance.

The Global Reporting Initiative (GRI) is the most well-known and often quoted standard for reporting on financial, environmental and social impacts. A good many Western listed companies now have at least some regard to the GRI when reporting. The GRI is welcome but in some respects remains in its infancy. Its origins lie in the environmental and, to a lesser degree, human rights movements. It is strong on environmental issues but tends to see social impact through the somewhat narrow lens of protecting against human rights violations and other regulatory compliance issues.

Other steps along the path to better integrated reporting are, however, also underway. For example, in South Africa the new corporate governance code established by King III requires listed companies, among other things, to report on their stakeholder relationships. Five major listed companies (including the largest mobile phone network provider in Africa, the second largest insurance group in South Africa, the state electricity and phone companies, and a big industrial and mining conglomerate) have participated in a pilot project to do just that. [32] They are identifying their key stakeholders, and are measuring, evaluating and reporting on the strength and quality of those relationships. Business needs a rational reason to be good. This information will provide that reason.

The second regulatory change necessary to support bi-productive investment is to require the investment management industry to advise its clients on the social and environmental implications of their investments and to obtain their views on these issues in the same way that the industry is currently required to discuss with clients their attitude to financial risk. This is perhaps no more than they should be doing already, since an understanding of financial, manufactured, human, intellectual, natural and social capital are all necessary if one is to understand the long-term viability of a business, but the focus should also be towards assessing the preferences of clients as regards social and environmental impacts as well as financial returns. A significant education process would be required to enable the industry to do this.

The investment management industry at present claims that clients are not interested in social and environmental impact. This is for a number of reasons. First, the industry lacks the necessary information; hence the need for integrated reporting. Second, the industry itself is not particularly interested, and it has little expertise in this field.

[32] The project is being run by Relationships Global in conjunction with the South African Institute of Directors and other corporate governance experts.

As a consequence, and as a defensive measure, it is dismissive of this motivation for investment and frames its inquiries of clients in a manner likely to lead to a negative response. In fact the opposite may be true. In a recent survey carried out for Nesta, financial planners were asked about the likelihood of their clients already having an interest in 'social impact investing', a far more rarefied form of investing to produce socially or environmentally beneficial outcomes. 75 per cent of planners believed there to be 'possibly' or 'highly likely' unidentified client demand for social impact investment among their clients. [33] It seems highly likely, therefore, that there is untapped interest amongst end-investors in the social and environmental consequences of their mainstream listed investments, particularly when it is understood that those consequences impact long-term financial performance. Third, the investment management industry seldom asks the individuals who are the ultimate end-owners of the capital it manages. It normally only talks to other financial services intermediaries.

So the third regulatory change needed to support bi-productive investment is to further democratise the investment process by requiring the industry to involve to a greater degree in the decisions made regarding their investments the individual investors who are the ultimate beneficial owners of all capital. The industry and its regulators may need to overcome their investment and regulatory paternalism to do so. Modern technology ought to make these kinds of connections possible, including by leaving room for intermediaries to play aggregating and advisory roles.

Armed with this information individual investors would, for example, be able to decide, based on the available information, to invest in a new manufacturing plant in the north west – in order to boost employment in that region – rather than to invest in a media business in the south east where the social benefits were less compelling and even though the financial returns were forecast to be the same or similar in both scenarios. They would be connected, when investing in a carbon intensive energy business, with the environmental costs of this form of energy provision, and might be more willing to invest next time around in a new clean energy provider with lower short-term financial returns but lower environmental externalities and better long-term prospects.

Investor democratisation might dramatically alter the landscape for stewardship. If the individual investors who own the funds managed on their behalf by pension funds and insurance companies were fully empowered to vote at company meetings, disquiet over issues such as Vodafone's tax avoidance or Barclays' director pay might lead to very different corporate behaviour.

The fourth regulatory change needed to support bi-productive investment is to require the investment management industry to report on the steps it itself is taking to engage with companies in relation to their social and environmental, as well as financial, performance. Those with the best track record may attract more clients.

[33] Nesta and Worthstone's report *Financial planners as catalysts for social investment* June 2012.

Conclusion

As mentioned above, the advantages of globalisation can be overstated. The bi-productive investment agenda is not, however, an anti-globalisation message. It is a pro-local connection message. Properly framed and properly supported by relevant information well presented to clients by advisors, it would produce a more socially sustainable form of globalisation; both local and global, not one or the other. Angel Gurria, the OECD secretary-general, has commented that the social contract is unravelling. It will not be mended, at least not in the West, unless we can find a genuine and fair justification for overturning, and the means and ways to overturn, the slide into high rates of unemployment caused by globalisation. Bi-productive investment, linked with the changes proposed in Chapters 2, 3 and 4, may help to achieve it. Free trade and globalisation have produced benefits for financial investors and consumers that previous generations have not needed to assess from the perspective of the redistribution of wealth to ensure a just society. Encouraging local investment is an important tool if we are to reverse the tide of the battle that is currently being won by global investors and consumers over national citizens and workers.

There would be costs associated with bi-productive investment. But the bigger picture might reveal, for example, lower UK taxes because of reduced social welfare bills, lower National Health Sector costs because of higher national wellbeing and stronger national GDP because of increases in local investment.

As investors, however, we will need to overcome our fears.

Man was born free but everywhere his investment advisor has tethered him to anxiety. There will be some investors who will lack the courage to depart from the conventional wisdom of a massively diversified investment portfolio, even though that strategy is not delivering on its diversification promise because of over correlation between markets. This over diversification makes it impossible for the investor to be interested in whether his capital is put to productive use.

IT'S ALL ABOUT THE MONEY

FUND MANAGER

FIND YOUR OWN THEN

CLIENT

There will also be some investors who will lack the courage to depart from the conventional wisdom of maximising financial return commensurate with risk, even though all that strategy is in fact producing, because of benchmarking, is simply the same return as everyone else, for better or worse. In fact, the net returns for the real end-owners of investments (savers and pensioners) are not encouraging, in part because of the fees charged by the investment management industry. If one takes into account the compound effect of fees and charges (such as entry fees, transaction charges, fund management fees, performance fees, withdrawal charges and possibly IFA or consultancy fees), as well as levels of inflation, many portfolios will produce very little real growth for real owners. Whilst the size of any specific fee may appear small as a percentage, the cumulative effect of the various layers of fees charged by the industry compounded over time is substantial. More often than not these fees reduce net returns to a level well below market benchmarks such as the FTSE 100. According to a report by The Royal Bank of Scotland[34], around 40 per cent of expected portfolio returns are currently being taken in fees, with expected net returns barely above inflation, if at all. After-tax returns will look even worse and returns adjusted for the appropriate cost of capital will often look positively paltry. So maybe bi-productive investment is not such a risk after all by comparison.

As many have remarked, our attitude to investing has historically been dominated by fear or greed, to one degree or another. Our isolationist, reductionist, utilitarian and controlling values make us poor investors. We do not want to look a fool either by doing worse than everyone else or by missing out on opportunities that might have made us richer. Our attempts as investors to measure, and therefore control, investment risk are in any event largely futile, not least because they focus on the short-term price of securities not the long-term value of businesses. The value at risk models beloved by the investment industry fail on a regular basis.

What if we decided instead that life was better when it was more of an adventure? Would we be more philosophical about any temporary setbacks in financial return, and more delighted by any unexpected financial successes? Would our savings and investments turn from being a hoard to be protected into a source of pleasure and surprise? If we decided to invest and wait patiently for long-term social, environmental and financial results would we be more released from quarterly reporting worry?

So the real challenge for bi-productive investment is not the regulatory reform that would be necessary to require companies to report on an integrated basis or any of the other reforms suggested in this Chapter. The real challenge is the change of heart and mind by end-investors.

The following Chapters provide some clues as to where we might find the energy and resolve to start making these changes, and those outlined in the previous Chapters, whether we are investors, investment managers, corporate directors or employees.

[34] *Financial Times* 26 September 2010.

6. A seedbed for change

Many have remarked that the City needs to recover a sense of morality and good character. One thing has been notable, however, from the many discussions about this that I have had in the City since the first wave of the financial crisis. And that is how little understanding there is about the connection between morality, character and behaviour. This is not to say that the City is immoral. It is to say that the City has, at least in part, misplaced its understanding of how morality operates, and of why it might be of benefit. Even using the word 'morality' immediately erects barriers in the minds of some. Morality well understood, however, simply describes the process by which we can make sound decisions about ourselves and the relationships that are the foundation of our society, including our economic relationships.

> *"We should remember that the most recent financial crisis did not emerge because practitioners did not know how to do maths. The issue is that few are trained to make good judgements, something that is well outside the scope of decision-trees and game theory. Quantitative analysis is but the beginning of sound business thinking. We shall have earned lasting benefit from the present strained conditions if we draw the lesson that historical context, ethical consideration and social ramifications warrant as much educational effort as the development of algorithmic skill."* [35]

There is no necessary conflict between morality and business. In fact the businesses that succeed in the long-term are generally those that are honest, committed to serving customers and hard working. These are all moral principles. Absent government bailouts, businesses that are economical with the truth, or that become interested only in themselves, go out of business. Another moral principle.

The Judeo/Christian understanding of morality, which still finds much resonance in the West, built on and adapted the Aristotelian understanding. It is first and foremost about the development of personal character. Classically the four virtues of courage, justice, wisdom and self-restraint identified by Aristotle are those that a person seeking to be moral needs to acquire through a lifetime of learning and practice. It is our characters that determine how we respond to ourselves and those around us. Character development is, therefore, both personal and social.

SELF RESTRAINT

[35] Hugh F Kelly, Clinical Associate Professor, NYU Schack Institute of Real Estate, New York, letter to the *Financial Times* 3 January 2012.

The Judeo/Christian tradition adds other virtues to the list, principally that of love but also faith and hope. For centuries this has provided the West with its cultural understanding about the proper use of power, and particularly the Western attachment to the idea that power should be used to benefit others rather than merely self. The paradox is that self is found through the denial of self for the benefit of others, and not through a process of self-absorption.

Character development is not a static affair. It is always a movement towards a purpose. For Aristotle, it was a movement towards a citizen fulfilling their potential, including by participating fully in political life. The concepts of human flourishing, the 'good life' and the common good reflect these ideas.

Deny or distort the purpose, the goal of the development, and the development becomes lost or diverted. This has been a particular mistake of Enlightenment philosophy as it has gathered pace over the last 250 years. The idea of a goal has been increasingly rejected because it seems on first analysis to limit the freedom of the individual. If I must be X then I cannot be Y. This misunderstands the nature of freedom, which is more constructively seen as freedom to flourish and become, not a freedom to stagnate or meander. This is why it is so important that business sets itself a clear purpose. Without it, values or even virtues have no energy – because they have no direction.

Character is not primarily about cultures and behaviours. These are the outcomes, not the source. It is our characters that determine how we act. Virtue asks primarily, 'who should I be?' The behavioural question 'what should I do?' then flows from who I am.

Character requires consistency. I am not moving towards having an honest character if I am regularly honest in one context but regularly dishonest in another. Under pressure, I am liable to be dishonest in both. Character needs to be instinctive, at least in measure, if it is to be fully trusted. Character is not theoretical. I cannot become compassionate if I do not practice compassion. Indeed, I cannot understand compassion if I do not practice compassion.

Alastair Cook is one of the finest cricketers of his generation; the only Englishman ever to score seven test centuries before his 23rd birthday. He is a joy to watch because of the hours that he has practiced and played. He reacts to a ball coming towards him at threatening speed with a mixture of intention and instinct. He is driven by a dual purpose: to bat well for himself and to do his team proud. His responses require courage and judgement in the moment, and the hours of prior practice that have taught his mind and body to react without seeming to think. And yet there is a clear intention as he steers the ball towards a chosen spot on the boundary. Character is the same; intuitive and intentional but only through practice.

Practicing virtue both gardens the soul and sharpens the conscience. Virtue based morality is not about ethics, if by that one means a system of self-regulation. Virtue can certainly constrain, but it is more focused on inspiration and freely made choices. Virtue understands the reason for the rule, and follows the reason not the regulation. Virtue becomes practiced at balancing, blending and prioritising competing but legitimate demands. Virtue takes the responsibility of choosing. It does not avoid responsibility by relying on regulations for which others carry responsibility, nor does it believe that by following the law virtue is necessarily being practiced.

Virtue provides an answer to the question "what do I do now?" when faced with an unfamiliar situation, and virtue provides the rationale for taking the harder route where necessary. Given that our knowledge of the available facts is more limited than we often suppose, and that our ability to calculate all of the consequences of our actions is more limited than we often care to admit, we are in reality faced with unfamiliar situations more frequently than we might imagine. In such situations, pragmatism often fails because it is so short sighted, and self-centeredness often fails because, if left to our own devices, we so easily swerve to self-destruction and become careless about the consequences of our choices on others.

Making decisions based on principle rather than pragmatism or regulation has a long-standing history. But it is also relevant in the current era. A few years ago The Institute of Chartered Accountants of Scotland set up a working group to examine the merits of various accounting methods. Their key recommendation was as follows:

> *"We support the consensus that only principles-based accounting standards can fully serve both the needs of business and the public interest."* [36]

Morality is not about standing in self-righteous judgement over the actions of others. It is about discerning and encouraging the beliefs and cultures that produce wellbeing, and discerning and discouraging those that result in harm. Take virtue out of the men and women who work in business and finance and you take virtue out of business and finance. Restore virtue in those who work in business and finance and you restore virtue in business and finance. Make business institutions focus on goals that are socially positive and you help those who work for them to be virtuous. Make financial institutions focus on goals that are socially damaging and you make it more difficult for those who work for them to be virtuous.

As we see every day, the cost of a lack of virtue is significant. To compensate for the shortfall we spend money on regulation, transparency, compliance, and accountability. Not to mention the worry and stress that enters our lives, and the lack of grace with which we start to treat each other, as we increasingly come to believe that others cannot be trusted.

[36] The Institute of Chartered Accountants of Scotland *Principles Not Rules, A Question of Judgement* 2006.

When confronted by slavery in the 19th century, and the vested interests in Parliament that were so reluctant to tackle what was evidently a moral outrage, William Wilberforce set out to make goodness fashionable. He did so on the basis that in the long run good policies are not simply good; they are also preferable. It is said that the banking crisis was a failure of character and competence. We desired the wrong destination, and we built the wrong ship. A refreshed sense of virtue and purpose are essential if we want to renew our bearings and set a new course.

How might businesses recognise and grow the kinds of people most likely to lead in accordance with these kinds of principles and virtues? Stephen Covey is the author of *The Seven Habits of Highly Effective People*, one of the world's bestselling leadership books. In his book *Principle-Centered Leadership* he describes the eight characteristics of people who lead by principle.

They are people who are constantly being educated by their experiences. They are curious and they listen to others.

They are people who see life as a mission not as a career. They wake up thinking of others.

They are people who are positive, hopeful and happy.

People who lead by principle are people who believe in others. They are not naïve but they can distinguish between the behaviour and the potential of others. They create a climate of possibility and forgive mistakes.

They are people who lead balanced lives. They are socially, intellectually and physically active. They have fun, and they are moderate not extreme.

They are people who see life as an adventure. Their security lies in their initiative and their resourcefulness, not in their safety or their protection. Others do not own them. They are not threatened by the fact that others are better than them in some ways.

They are people who are synergistic. They see that the whole is more than the sum of the parts. They find solutions that benefit everyone.

And finally, people who lead by principle are people who take deliberate steps for self-renewal. They exercise daily the four dimensions of the human personality: physical, mental, emotional and spiritual.

These are the characteristics that we must foster and celebrate if we are to produce business leaders with character and purpose.

7. Early years

If we want sound finances we need sound families. The family may seem a strange place in which to locate a foundation stone for business. But the family is vital for two reasons. First, the family is the place where we learn to be inter-connected humans. And, second, the family is the place where we first learn about economics.

Self-worth

It is within the family that our sense of self-worth develops most as we appreciate the unconditional love of others, based not on our looks or our abilities but simply on our being. Families teach us that we are valued despite our eccentricities and shortcomings.

It is this self-worth, properly formed, that protects us in later life, including in business, from the need to over perform, seek approval from bosses or customers, or hide our mistakes from colleagues or investors. It is this sense of self-worth that protects us from the need to avoid difficult decisions and conversations, that protects us from the need to be aggressive towards others who may challenge us, and that enables us to make decisions based on compassion and reason rather than fear and greed.

In families we learn that true relaxation comes as we live integrated rather than disjointed lives. In families we appreciate the value of being accepted for who we truly are, rather than for the appearance that we might choose to adopt in more public spaces. The family may not make us happy, but it gives us reason to be happy.

In families we learn the connection between personal freedom and personal boundaries. We learn that freedom without boundaries does not lead to happiness or fulfilment. We learn that it leads instead to self-destruction and a lack of direction. We learn that real freedom comes as we move from externally imposed rules to internally generated limits; as we learn how to be free from our unhelpful passions and appetites, and learn instead how to be free to pursue our talents and dreams. We learn that maximising our pleasure and avoiding any pain, a key maxim of contemporary economics, in fact leads to obesity and weakness not focus and achievement. We learn that constant accumulation in response to externally generated desire is both pointless and endless.

We learn in families how morality, rather than being a tiresome restraint, in fact helps us to become ourselves.

Relationships

It is within the family that we also learn the truth of the African wisdom: *"I am because you are"*.

In families we learn about inter-dependence. We see that no man is an island. We learn that our existence depends on the contributions of others, as theirs does on ours. We learn the paradox of relationships – for example that it is only as we give love that we can receive it in return. We learn that we are stronger and more productive together than we are alone. We learn the combination of giving dignity to the individual and appreciating the benefits of the communal. Families are not reductionist, they are holistic.

In families we learn that regard only for self is not only a moral and emotional mistake, but also an intellectual mistake. We learn about loyalty, truthfulness and forgiveness, and their effect on others as well as on ourselves. In families the success of the one need not threaten the worth of another.

Families teach us that the freedom of others, to be and to flourish, depends on our accepting limits on our own behaviour. Families teach us about systemic thinking. We learn that our actions have consequences on others, and that we need to accept responsibility for the consequences of those actions. In families we learn that rest and reflection are necessary if we are to understand ourselves, and our effects on others. In families we learn how to resolve rather than escalate disagreements.

We learn in families that a 'rational' and self-centred individual seeking only to maximise his wealth and minimise his costs forms a poor basis for a harmonious community. We learn how to find solutions that benefit all, not just the strong, or even just the majority.

We learn in families how morality helps a society to operate for the benefit of all. We learn that morality is simply the set of freely chosen beliefs and values that determines the nature and quality of our behaviours and cultures. We learn that morality is a word that describes how to make relationships work well for the benefit of all.

THE FAMILY

Economics

The magic of families, however, is that they also teach us much about economics.

First of all, families keep economics in its rightful place. Family life is about much more than economics. It is also about health, education, community and fun. It is also about celebration, relaxation, creativity and spirituality.

The purpose of economics within a family is to provide an outlet for endeavour and a source of revenue for life. In families finance serves a purpose, the family does not serve finance. Families do not make decisions based solely on the prospects for economic growth. They adopt a more balanced scorecard approach.

Families also teach us much about the nature and diversity of economic relationships.

Within a family some are earning and some are dependent. Not everyone is economically productive in the same way, or at all. But everyone has a place at the table.

Families think about finance on a long-term and inter-generational basis. Each generation makes sacrifices for the benefit of its children and grandchildren, and each generation tries to ensure that the one that follows is left with greater resources than the one that went before. Families teach us the benefit of combining masculine and feminine characteristics in problem analysis and decision making processes.

In families, no one is measuring the contribution of one as opposed to the contribution of another. It is not just that some are contributing a wage and others are helping with the washing-up. There is no contract that balances one person's contribution against the contribution of another, even after allowing for age and ability. Instead each contributes, without counting, knowing that in the long run everyone benefits.

Families are economic units based on mutual gifts not individual rights. They do not see life as a zero sum game where my gain can only be achieved as a result of your loss.

Indeed, families teach us that true wealth is not found in riches at all. It is found in relationships on which we can rely. Families teach us about the difference between sufficiency and accumulation. If my family's plenty may supply my need I need not store up possessions against every possible disaster. I become more relaxed about economics based on enough rather than more.

Families recognise the particular financial responsibilities that exist for those who are relationally closest. Families are part of larger communities and seek to be generous, financially and in other ways, to those beyond the immediate family. However, they do this without threatening the financial sustainability or cohesiveness of the family itself. Families recognise that in this globalised world everyone is a neighbour, but they do not exhaust their resources and fail to look after their own. They recognise that often what the neighbour needs is not a gift but protection from the over-mighty and the self-belief and opportunity to look after themselves.

In families we learn about the subtleties of different types of property ownership. We learn that private property is not a monochrome concept. We learn that some things are mine and can never be used by another, that some things are mine and can be used by another with consent (and that that consent cannot be unreasonably withheld) and we learn that some things are mine and can be used by another with no need first to gain consent because there are legitimate communal expectations about the use of that property.

Families are economic realists. Theories of finance mean little unless they are practical. Families do not live in economic ivory towers.

Families teach us that morality is relational and practical. If we ever find ourselves being tempted to become unrelational, or to give precedence to social theories or bureaucratic arrangements over their human implications, it is likely that we are being tempted to become less than moral. In families the structure serves the family, not the family the structure.

If we want sound finances we need sound families. Everything is connected.

8. Building cathedrals

The finance industry cannot be mended in isolation from the society of which it is a part. To believe that it can is to repeat the mistake of reductionism. As with a team of horses pulling a carriage, one horse cannot run ahead of the others but they can all run faster if they all run faster together. The cultures and behaviours of the finance industry will only reform to the extent and as quickly as each of the other spheres of society. For the finance industry to change politics, education, the media, the arts and the family must also change.

In politics we will need more integrity, less pretence of control, and decision making based on national wellbeing not simply economics. Our educational model will need to become one of relational intelligence and practical experience as well as academic credentials. The media will need to abandon sensationalised and polarised argument and embrace truthfulness and balanced decision making. The arts will need to make heroes of those who practice purposeful business and finance. And families will need to grow young men and women who are emotionally secure and aware of their unique talents.

In the meantime, those who work in the finance industry who wish to see change might like to consider the following practical steps to hasten that change:

- avoid exhaustion, in particular by not working every evening and every weekend,
- take time out regularly to reflect, preferably in the countryside,
- treasure your family,
- discuss some of the themes in this book with others, first of all with friends and then with colleagues,
- exercise leadership over your own sphere of influence, however modest or informal that might be, and starting with yourself,
- seek out and partner with others seeking a similar change, including by identifying the good business reasons for change,
- do not despise small beginnings, and be prepared for both patience and action,
- engage with someone who is poor, not as a volunteer but as a friend,
- invest some money, and something of yourself, in a UK social impact investment, and
- take a journey to a low income country to explore the difference that micro and SME business makes to a developing economy.

However, we also need institutional reform to enable us to put into practice the good principles to which we aspire. The financial system, in particular, has taken on too many policies and practices that work against our best interests. We need structural reform to help us become more relational, more holistic, more neighbourly, more adventurous, more purposeful, more humble and more principled. That is why I am suggesting the steps outlined in the previous Chapters.

This would, of course, be a long and difficult journey.

The foundation stone for the Basilica di Santa Maria del Fiore, Florence's magnificent cathedral and better known as the Duomo, was laid in 1291. On top stands a dome that is 143 feet in diameter. Until the 20th century it was the widest and tallest dome in Europe, but the shape of the dome was not settled until 76 years after the first foundation stone was laid.

Although the shape was settled in 1367, still no one had any idea as to how the dome was actually going to be built. And yet the masons had started, and continued, with their work, financed by the people of Florence. No dome of that size had ever been built before, and it was recognised that even their most advanced building methods were not up to the task. In particular, they knew that the span of the dome was too great to allow it to be built using wooden centering to hold up the dome during construction. This did not deter the Florentines. They carried on building, and each year the master craftsmen working on site swore an oath to complete the dome in accordance with the design finalised in 1367. It was not for another 50 years that Filippo Brunelleschi won a competition to build the dome – 126 years after construction had started. Work on the dome itself started in 1418. At that point still no one, other than Brunelleschi, knew how the dome was to be constructed. He had won the competition without revealing his secrets. 13 years later the dome was completed, without wooden centering.

Sometimes it is necessary to start building with a dream in mind and then continue with patience, faith and determination. Sometimes one may not necessarily know how to complete the task, but one can be guided by purpose and principle and allow for the possibility that it may fall to others to complete the task.

BUILDING CATHEDRALS

"Thence we came forth to rebehold the stars."

Dante Alighieri *Divine Comedy* 1321

ICAEW

The Institute of Chartered Accountants in England and Wales is professional membership organisation, supporting over 138,000 chartered accountants around the world. Through our technical knowledge, skill and expertise, we provide insight and leadership to the global accountancy and finance profession. Our members provide financial knowledge and guidance based on the highest professional, technical and ethical standards. We develop and support individuals, organisations and communities to help them achieve long-term sustainable economic value.

www.icaew.com

LICC

Since its founding in 1982 the London Institute for Contemporary Christianity has been supporting Christians in all spheres of daily life and assisting with the dialogue between spirituality and the workplace. Historically, and today, a Christian understanding of the purpose of business and finance in the service of the individual and common good has provided robust, productive and practical frameworks for praxis and profit, as well as restraint and control, and we are delighted to co-publish this compelling contribution to the vital and urgent question of how we reshape business and finance for a richer (in every sense of the word) and more liberating future for all.

www.licc.org.uk

Tomorrow's Company

Tomorrow's Company is the agenda setting 'think and do' tank which looks at the role of business and how to achieve enduring business success. We focus on strong relationships, clear purpose and values as the foundation of effective leadership and governance. In our programmes we challenge business leaders around the world to work in dialogue with others to tackle the toughest issues. We promote systemic solutions, working across boundaries between business, investors, government and society. We believe that business can and must be a 'force for good'. This in turn requires a strengthening of stewardship by shareholders *in partnership with boards of companies*. We argue that the Age of Sustainability has begun, and that in the future success and value creation will come from recognising the 'triple context' – the links between the economic, social and environmental sub-systems on which we all depend, and the opportunities this brings.

www.tomorrowscompany.com